LIFE INSURANCE TRENDS AT MID-CENTURY

THE S. S. HUEBNER FOUNDATION FOR INSURANCE EDUCATION

David McCahan, *Editor*

Lectures

LIFE INSURANCE: TRENDS AND PROBLEMS

THE BENEFICIARY IN LIFE INSURANCE

LIFE INSURANCE TRENDS AT MID-CENTURY

Studies

AN ANALYSIS OF GOVERNMENT LIFE INSURANCE

AN ANALYSIS OF GROUP LIFE INSURANCE

LIFE INSURANCE TRENDS
AT
MID-CENTURY

Edited by

David McCahan, Ph.D., (C.L.U.)

Executive Director
The S. S. Huebner Foundation
for Insurance Education

Philadelphia
UNIVERSITY OF PENNSYLVANIA PRESS

LONDON: GEOFFREY CUMBERLEGE
OXFORD UNIVERSITY PRESS
1950

THE S. S. HUEBNER FOUNDATION FOR INSURANCE EDUCATION

The S. S. Huebner Foundation for Insurance Education was created in 1940, under the sponsorship of a Cooperating Committee representing the life insurance institution, to aid in strengthening insurance education on the collegiate level. It functions along three principal lines:

1. Providing fellowships and scholarships to aid teachers in accredited colleges and universities of the United States and Canada, or persons who are contemplating a teaching career in such colleges and universities, to secure preparation at the graduate level for insurance teaching and research.
2. Building up and maintaining a research service center in insurance books and other source material which will be available through circulating privileges to teachers in accredited colleges and universities desirous of conducting research in insurance subjects.
3. Publishing research theses and other studies which constitute a distinct contribution directly or indirectly to insurance knowledge.

The activities of the Foundation are under the direction of an Administrative Board consisting of six officers and faculty members of the University of Pennsylvania and two faculty members of other universities.

PREFACE

Legal reserve life insurance, viewed at the midpoint of the Twentieth Century, is closely interwoven with the fabric of the economic and social systems of the United States and Canada. Embracing virtually half the population as owners of its life insurance and annuity contracts, providing a modern instrument for meeting the age-old and inborn quest for economic security, and holding in a fiduciary capacity more than sixty billions of dollars in assets, it has attained size and significance unparalleled elsewhere in the world. Because it is dynamic, it has helped to shape the direction in which the pattern of life has evolved, at the same time being shaped by its own environment. As a part of American life, it has been confronted with all of the manifold problems which epidemics, wars, depressions, social conflicts, political philosophies and scientific discoveries have produced. It is still in the process of evolution and the trends to which this volume relates bear testimony to its vitality and its powers of adaptation.

The presentation of a volume such as this is in conformity with the policy established by the Administrative Board of The S. S. Huebner Foundation for Insurance Education, which places considerable emphasis upon the publication of material that will be especially useful to college or university teachers of insurance in their instructional work. As elsewhere stated, this publication policy has been influenced by the following primary considerations:

(1) The conviction that every teacher who keeps faith with the ideals of his profession wants to be fully informed on all matters of consequence in the realm of his specialty.

(2) The realization that college and university instruction in insurance has already reached, and will continue to reach, far more students in the broad domain of economics, government,

sociology and their subdivisions than in such specialized voca-
tional subjects as insurance law, actuarial science and insurance
medicine.

(3) The recognition that a teacher in the social science subjects
must obtain a broad comprehension of the life insurance institution as a whole in its social setting. This must be an "over-all"
view which not only includes the structure, functions and services of this institution but also its manifold interrelationships
with other institutions which make up American life today.

(4) The realization that analysis and thorough study of all the
technical literature in life insurance is a time-consuming process
which is frequently prohibitive for the teacher whose duties require that he have an equally broad grasp of other important
economic and social institutions. To keep himself conversant
with all the developments and the new ideas which are presented
in the journals of the actuarial societies, the medical directors,
the agency executives, the insurance lawyers, the life underwriters, etc., and to be reasonably well informed on matters of
importance which have not been there presented, is no small task.

Thus far, the Foundation has undertaken the issuance of two
series of volumes, known as "Huebner Foundation Lectures" and
"Huebner Foundation Studies," the first series comprising a compilation of addresses on selected insurance topics and the second
presenting the results of thorough research in specific areas. This
is the third volume in the "Lectures" series. As was the case with
its predecessors, it contains a series of lectures given under the
auspices of the Foundation at the University of Pennsylvania.
Each of the lectures in the present series was delivered at a dinner
meeting attended by fellows and scholars of the Foundation and
teachers from the Insurance Department faculty. In following this
procedure, members of the Foundation's Administrative Board
had in mind the desirability of enabling these present and future
teachers of insurance to enjoy the privilege of hearing outstanding
authorities, with a background of broad experience in the life
insurance field, discuss the subjects assigned to them. The primary directing principle followed in the selection of the speakers
was their capacity to make a worth-while contribution to the
thinking of this teaching group.

Publication of these manuscripts was authorized by the Administrative Board of the Foundation with the sincere hope, and in the confident belief, that their range of usefulness might be extensively widened through making them available to other teachers and students of insurance who could not hear the original presentation. It was felt that such publication would be in full accord with the policy above set forth.

As was the case with the first two volumes of lectures, this one is of significance, not alone because of the high standing in the life insurance world of those who have made it possible and the inherent quality of their respective contributions to it, but because it reflects the continuance of an organized effort to provide a literature especially intended for teachers in the broad field of the social sciences. Conscious as these teachers are of the complexities and ramifications of the subjects with which they deal and the frequent inconclusiveness of the researches therein, they are nevertheless zealous to broaden their understanding and enrich their teaching. To them this volume is dedicated. Through them it is hoped that research may be stimulated. From them will be welcomed substantial participation in the subsequent studies, monographs and other materials which are published under the auspices of this Foundation.

To each of the various lecturers whose name appears in the Table of Contents and in the specific chapter which he prepared, and who has helped to make this volume possible by his gracious, competent and generous participation, and to Miss Mary Drever who has rendered valuable editorial assistance, the editor acknowledges his deep indebtedness and hearty appreciation.

It should in no wise detract from the quality of the volume to point out that expressions of opinion which may appear in publications of the Huebner Foundation are those of the authors and not of the Foundation itself.

D. McC.

Philadelphia
September 1950

CONTENTS

CHAPTER   PAGE

PREFACE   vii

I   THE IMPACT OF LOWER INTEREST EARNINGS, *by* A. A. Rydgren   1

    Impact on New Policies   3
      High Premium Participating Companies   4
      Low Premium Participating Companies   5
      Nonparticipating Companies   5
    Impact on Old Policies   6
      Net Costs   7
      Reserve Strengthening   11
    Impact on Settlement Options   14
      In New Policies   14
      In Old Policies   16
    Policy Loan Interest   17
    Conclusion   17

II   IMPLICATIONS OF THE GUERTIN LEGISLATION, *by* Henry H. Jackson   19

    By Way of Introduction   19
    Life Insurance in the United States   20
    The Objectives of Insurance Supervision   21
    Something about Reserves   22
    The Full Net Level Premium Method   23
    A More Realistic Reserve Method   24
    Something about Nonforfeiture Values   25
    The New Statutory Measure of Nonforfeiture Values   27
    Achievements of the New Legislation   28
    Desiderata Beyond Statutory Requirements   29
    The Situation in 1948   30
    A Suggested Comparison   31

III   INVESTMENT TRENDS AND PROBLEMS, *by* James J. O'Leary   33

    Investment Trends Since 1940   35
      The War Period   35
      The Postwar Period   35

CHAPTER		PAGE
	Investment Problems	37
	The Equity Capital Problem	37
	The Problem of Declining Interest Rates	40
	Some Problems Involved in Stock Investments	41
	Some Problems Involved in Direct Investment in Rental Housing	43
	The Purchase of Income-producing Real Estate and Lease-back	44
	Other Problems	45
IV	PRINCIPLES AND PROBLEMS OF SELECTION AND UNDERWRITING, *by* Pearce Shepherd	47
	Fundamental Principles of Underwriting	47
	Underwriting Procedures and the Factors Influencing Mortality	50
	Provision for Extra Mortality	51
	Summary of General Principles	54
	Other Underwriting Problems	54
	Recent Developments	56
	Insurable Interest and Finances	63
	Conclusion	66
V	REINSURANCE OF LIFE RISKS, *by* Walter O. Menge	68
	Retention Limits	69
	Reinsurance Procedure	73
	Reinsurance Plans	75
	General Reinsurance Provisions	79
	Reinsurance Situation Today	82
VI	SIGNIFICANT ANNUITY DEVELOPMENTS, *by* Ray D. Murphy	84
	Historical Background	84
	Recent Growth of Annuity Contracts	85
	The Character of Current Annuity Contracts	89
	I. Individual Contracts	89
	Immediate Annuities: Life Annuity; Refund Annuity;	89
	Cash Refund Annuity; Joint and Survivor Annuity	90
	Deferred Annuities: Single Premium Deferred Annuity;	90
	Annual Premium Deferred Annuity	90
	II. Group Annuity Contracts	91
	Unit Annuity Plan	93
	Money Purchase Plan	93
	Deposit Administration Plan	94
	Company Problems in Conducting the Annuity Business	95

CHAPTER   PAGE

VII   DEVELOPMENT OF DISABILITY BENEFITS IN LIFE INSUR-
ANCE CONTRACTS, *by* Joseph B. Maclean   100

Developments up to 1932   100
Changes Made in 1932   103
Developments from 1932 to 1948   104
Current Practice   108
Future Developments   109
Proposed Extension of O.A.S.I.   111
Summary of Benefits of 30 Large Companies   112

VIII   MODERN INDUSTRIAL LIFE INSURANCE, *by* Malvin E.
Davis   115

Policy Provisions   118
Selection of Risks   121
Field Force Organization   122
Premium Accounting System   122
Selection and Training of Agents   123
Agents' Compensation   124
Family Programming   125
    Relation of Premiums to Family Income   125
    Distribution of Insurance within the Family   126
    Frequency of Premium Payment   127
    Plans of Insurance   127
Persistency   128
Health and Welfare Work   129
Expense   130
Recent Trends in Wage-Earners' Insurance   132

IX   THE GROWING FIELD OF GROUP COVERAGES, *by* Henry
S. Beers   133

A Particular Group Plan   135
Announcement Letter   135
Schedule of Insurance Benefits   136
Description of the Plan   137
    Eligibility   137
    Life Insurance   139
    Accidental Death and Dismemberment Benefits   140
    Sickness and Accident Benefits   140
    Hospital Benefits for Employees   141
    Surgical Benefits for Employees   143
    Medical Expense Benefits for Employees   143
    Dependents' Hospital Benefits   144
    Dependents' Surgical Benefits   145

CONTENTS

CHAPTER   PAGE

No Medical Examination 146
Insurance Certificate 146
Payment of Claims 147
Termination of Insurance 147
Effective Date 147
Schedule of Operations 148
Premium Rates 150
Recent Collective Bargaining Developments 151
History 152

X RESEARCH IN AGENCY MANAGEMENT, *by* Charles J. Zimmerman 156

Role of the Agency Management Association 157
Selection 159
Training 161
Supervision 162
Morale 164
Job Satisfaction 165
Compensation 165
Other Research 167
Significant Trends 168

INDEX 171

LIFE INSURANCE TRENDS AT MID-CENTURY

CHAPTER I

THE IMPACT OF LOWER INTEREST EARNINGS

By A. A. Rydgren, F.S.A.*

Nothing that has happened during the past twenty years—a period including the great depression of the 1930's as well as World War II, a period marked by extreme social and political unrest—has affected life insurance in the United States so deeply or so enduringly as has the concurrent drop in the interest rate. The direct result of lower interest earnings has been an increase in premium rates, a substantial increase in the net cost to a policyholder of providing a given face amount of life insurance for his family and the even much greater increase in the cost of providing a given income for it. These results seem likely to endure for a long time, perhaps permanently.

The interest rate is fundamental to the structure of life insurance. Premiums, reserves and most policy guarantees are computed on the assumption of a specific rate of interest. It is assumed that such specific rate of interest will be earned on the reserve each and every year as long as the policy remains in force. The life insurance company expects to receive such interest as well as the premiums in order that it may meet policy claims and expenses. After a policy has been put into effect, the company is powerless to increase the premium even though interest earnings become less than expected at the time when the policy was issued. When, therefore, the interest rate drops from 5 per cent, the rate earned in 1930 and for many years prior thereto, to 2.8 per cent earned in 1947, the effect on life insurance is indeed profound.

To illustrate exactly what has happened to the interest rate earned on life company funds, Table I shows the average net rate of interest earned, according to Best's Life Insurance Reports, by the ten largest life insurance companies of the United States

* Chairman of the Board, Continental American Life Insurance Company.

ranked by assets as of December 31, 1940. These are the same companies used for the same purpose in my paper "The Significance of Reduced Interest Earnings" which was presented seven years ago and published in the 1943 volume of the Huebner Foundation lectures entitled *Life Insurance: Trends and Problems.*

TABLE I

Average Net Rate of Interest Earned by Ten Largest Companies

Year	Per Cent
1928	5.0
1929	5.0
1930	5.0
1931	4.9
1932	4.7
1933	4.2
1934	3.9
1935	3.7
1936	3.7
1937	3.7
1938	3.6
1939	3.5
1940	3.4
1941	3.4
1942	3.3
1943	3.3
1944	3.1
1945	3.1
1946	2.9
1947	2.8

These ten companies are:

Ordinary Participating Companies
Equitable Life (New York)
Mutual Benefit
Mutual (New York)
New York Life
Northwestern Mutual
Penn Mutual

Ordinary and Industrial Participating Companies
John Hancock
Metropolitan
Prudential

Ordinary Non-Participating Company
Travelers

The loss in interest earnings has reached tremendous proportions. For the year 1947 alone, on the mean assets of the 228 life insurance companies in the United States included in the compilation of the *Unique Manual-Digest,* a loss of 2.2 per cent aggregates over $1,100,000,000. This loss is twice the total of policy dividends such companies distributed that year.

Despite this huge loss in interest earnings, the surplus position of the life companies is almost as good as it was twenty years ago. To illustrate, the ratio of capital, surplus and contingency reserves to liabilities of the ten largest companies (those included in Table I) averaged 6.94 per cent as of December 31, 1928 and averaged 6.31 per cent as of December 31, 1947. The drastic reduction in the rate of interest earnings has had no significant effect on the current financial position of these companies.

The companies have met the challenge of lower interest earnings by taking measures which have kept their financial strength intact. This paper, therefore, deals largely with those measures and how such measures affect policyholders.

IMPACT ON NEW POLICIES

Although the solution of the problem relating to new insurance was quite simple, nevertheless the life insurance companies were most reluctant to adopt the obvious solution, namely, the assumption of a lower rate of interest for the accumulation of reserves and the adoption of a higher scale of premiums. It is probably true that the higher the premium the more difficult it is for the average man to carry adequate life insurance, even though the net cost of carrying such life insurance is reduced after a year or two by the application of policy dividends. When the interest assumption for the calculation of reserves is lowered, it is always true, other things being equal, that it becomes more difficult to carry the same amount of life insurance. The reason is that when such interest rate is lowered, policy reserves and cash values increase, and if policy claims, expenses and other factors be the same, then the net amount paid by the policyholder, premiums less policy dividends, must be greater to the extent of the increase in policy reserves. Although the people of the United States own most of the life insurance in force in the world, only a small proportion of them seems able to carry an adequate amount of life insurance. It is but natural, therefore, that the life insurance companies were reluctant to increase premium rates or to lower the interest assumption for the accumulation of reserves and, in my judgment, the companies were distinctly on the late side in taking these corrective measures.

The problem with respect to new policies has, moreover, been quite different for different companies. Companies which had been issuing new policies on the assumption that reserves would be accumulated at 3½ per cent interest were under more pressure to reduce the interest assumption for new policies than were companies which were already on the 3 per cent interest basis. Companies with a low premium scale, those issuing non-participating insurance and those issuing participating insurance at low participating premium rates containing little or no margin in excess of a minimum policy dividend, were under greater pressure to increase premium rates than were those companies which issued participating insurance at a high premium scale containing very much larger margins for policy dividends.

The measures taken by the ten companies whose experience is included in Table I illustrate how differently situated companies solved the problem with respect to new insurance.

High Premium Participating Companies. The six Ordinary Participating Companies may all be considered for this purpose as having been high premium participating companies twenty years ago. In 1929, for example, these six companies computed premiums and reserves on a 3 per cent interest basis, and gross premiums for ordinary life insurance issued at age 35 varied from a low of $26.35 per thousand to a high of $28.11 per thousand, averaging $27.32 per thousand. None of these companies changed its premium scale or interest assumption for the accumulation of reserves until 1944 when one of the companies reduced such interest assumption to 2½ per cent, leaving its premium scale unchanged for ordinary life policies. The other five companies in this group made no such change until they were ready to adopt new rates and values based on the new Commissioners' Standard Ordinary Table of Mortality which became mandatory on January 1, 1948. At the present time these companies charge premiums for ordinary life insurance issued at age 35 varying from a low of $27.61 per thousand to a high of $29.40, with an average of $28.44. At the present time one of these companies assumes 2½ per cent interest for the accumulation of reserves on new policies, three assume $2\frac{1}{4}$ per cent, and two assume 2 per cent interest. It is interesting to note that one of these companies, one which reduced its interest assumption to $2\frac{1}{2}$ per cent in 1944 and then to 2 per cent late in 1947, still continues its old premium scale for ordinary life policies.

Low Premium Participating Companies. The three companies described as Ordinary and Industrial Participating Companies may have been regarded as low premium participating companies twenty years ago. In 1929, for example, their premiums for ordinary life insurance at age 35 varied from a low of $21.40 per thousand to a high of $25.88, averaging $23.83. At that time each of these companies assumed $3\frac{1}{2}$ per cent interest for the accumulation of policy reserves on new policies. These companies began increasing premiums for new insurance as early as 1935. During this period of falling interest rates, each of these companies has made at least two increases in premium rates. At the present time each of these three companies assumes $2\frac{1}{2}$ per cent interest for the accumulation of reserves under new policies, and new premiums for ordinary life insurance at age 35 vary from a low of $25.00 per thousand to a high of $28.75, averaging $26.38.

Nonparticipating Companies. There is only one such company included in Table I, though in my judgment it is a typical nonparticipating company. Twenty years ago, this company accumulated reserves at $3\frac{1}{2}$ per cent interest, charging a premium for ordinary life insurance at age 35, of $19.71 per thousand. It has likewise made a succession of changes, both lowering the interest assumption for the accumulation of reserves and increasing premiums for new insurance. At the present time it is issuing new policies on a $2\frac{1}{2}$ per cent interest assumption for the accumulation of reserves and is charging for ordinary life insurance at age 35 a premium of $22.24.

Almost all of the increase in premium rates is due to the reduction in the rate of interest earned on life insurance funds. While it is true that present premium scales are based on a different mortality table—the Commissioners' Standard Ordinary Table of Mortality instead of the American Experience Table of Mortality—and while some companies may have provided larger margins for expenses as the result of the depreciation in the purchasing power of the dollar, nevertheless it would seem correct to state that the effect of these two factors on premium rates has been quite insignificant. There is every reason to believe that substantially the whole of the increase in premiums during this period has been due to the fall in the interest rate.

It is interesting to observe that one of the results of these changes has been a narrowing of the spread between the premium scales in use by the various companies. Twenty years ago, the premiums charged by these ten companies for ordinary life insurance at age 35 varied from a low of $19.71 to a high of $28.11, the spread being $8.40. Now such premiums vary from a low of $22.24 to a high of $29.40, the spread being reduced to $7.16. On the average, participating premiums now contain less margin for policy dividends than did the premiums of twenty years ago.

It is interesting to note, too, how narrow is the present margin between the rate of interest earned and the rate assumed for the accumulation of reserves in new policies. Twenty years ago, when the companies were earning 5 per cent interest, reserves on new policies were being accumulated at either $3\frac{1}{2}$ per cent interest or 3 per cent interest, leaving a margin of excess interest ranging from $1\frac{1}{2}$ per cent to 2 per cent. Now when the companies are earning only 2.8 per cent interest, according to the most recent experience available, namely, that of 1947, new policies are being issued on the basis of accumulating reserves at a rate of interest varying from 2 per cent to $2\frac{1}{2}$ per cent—the present margin of excess interest varying from 0.3 per cent to 0.8 per cent. The present narrow margin of excess interest earnings is concrete evidence of the reluctance of the life insurance companies to go all the way in reflecting the actual recent interest rate experience in the terms at which new policies are being issued.

Impact on Old Policies

The problems created by the fall in the interest rate have been much more difficult to solve for old insurance. Life insurance policies are exceedingly long term contracts. A large proportion of them cover the whole period of life. Moreover, most of the old policies guarantee settlement options under which the proceeds at death or maturity may be left with the company under guarantees which are far more liberal than are justified by recent interest and mortality experience. After a policy has been put in force, the company has no power either to increase the premium rate or to diminish any of the policy guarantees. As a result, some old policies are now being carried at a loss to the companies.

With respect to old policies, too, not all companies were affected alike. The lower the premium rates and the higher the rate of interest at which reserves were being accumulated, the more severely was old insurance affected by the fall in the interest rate and the more drastic was the remedy called for. The companies were more severely affected under nonparticipating insurance than under participating insurance because under participating policies the lower interest earnings could be offset, at least partially if not entirely, by lower policy dividends; but under nonparticipating policies, regardless of subsequent actual experience, the annual net cost is the annual premium and it is fixed at the outset.

Net Costs. On participating policies, policy dividends were promptly adjusted downward in probably all companies which issued such policies. Table II shows the twenty year net cost per $1,000 of the ten largest participating companies, excluding industrial companies, doing business in the state of New York. These are the net costs for an ordinary life policy issued at age 35 based on the then current premium and dividend scales.

The companies included in Table II are the six Ordinary Participating companies included in Table I together with the Massachusetts Mutual, New England Mutual, Connecticut Mutual and Provident Mutual. Incidentally, the eleventh largest such company is included instead of the tenth largest because such data for the tenth largest company are not published.

For the benefit of those who may want to know exactly how the figures in Table II have been computed, each figure is the unweighted average for the ten companies. The net costs in column (1) represent twenty annual premiums less policy dividends up to and including that payable at the end of the twentieth policy year. Each figure in column (3) is the difference between that in column (1) and column (2) computed to dollars and cents but shown to the nearest dollar.

The outstanding fact revealed by Table II is that according to the 1948 premium and dividend scale, it costs a policyholder $75 more, or 21 per cent more, to maintain such a policy in force for twenty years than it did according to the 1929 premium and

TABLE II

AVERAGE TWENTY YEAR NET COST PER $1,000 OF TEN LARGEST
PARTICIPATING ORDINARY COMPANIES

Year of Issue	(1) Net Cost for 20 Years (Premiums less dividends)	(2) Cash Value End of 20 Years	(3) 20 Year Surrendered Net Cost (Premiums less dividends less cash value)
1929	$353	$325	$28
1930	353	325	28
1931	354	325	29
1932	362	325	37
1933	378	325	52
1934	400	325	75
1935	403	327	76
1936	408	327	81
1937	408	327	81
1938	406	327	79
1939	410	327	83
1940	408	327	81
1941	416	327	89
1942	419	327	92
1943	422	327	95
1944	422	329	93
1945	417	331	86
1946	418	336	82
1947	413	341	72
1948	428	371	57
Increase in Net Cost (1929-48)	75		29

dividend scale. In other words, there has been an annual increase of $3.75 per $1,000 in the net cost of maintaining such an ordinary life policy in force.

Table II also reveals that part of such increase in the net cost of maintaining such a policy in force is due to the increase in the cash value which, at the end of the twentieth year, approximates the policy reserve. If the policy be surrendered at the end of twenty years, the surrendered net cost according to the 1948 scale is only $29 more than that according to the 1929 scale, or only

$1.45 per thousand per year. Incidentally, while these surrendered net costs are computed according to the formula commonly used by life insurance agents when in competition, this formula does not produce scientifically accurate results because it ignores the important factor of interest on the difference in yearly net costs during the twenty years. The error inherent in such formulae is part of the explanation as to why surrendered net costs have been decreasing during the last five years while net costs to continuing policyholders have even increased slightly, the last five years being the period when the companies have been most active in reducing the interest rate for the accumulation of reserves on new policies, thus increasing the twentieth year cash values thereof.

The really serious difficulties encountered by the companies in reducing dividend scales applicable to many old policies are not, however, revealed by Table II. Lower interest earnings have resulted not only in smaller policy dividends but in a complete change in the pattern of the scale of policy dividends. As long as the rate of interest earned on life company funds remained comfortably above 4 per cent, as it did during the whole history of life insurance in the United States prior to 1930, policy earnings and, therefore, policy dividends tended to increase with the increase in policy duration as long as the same dividend scale was maintained. Thus, all past experience confirmed the policyholder in his expectation that dividends on his policy would increase from year to year, except on the rare occasions when adverse experience required a reduction in the dividend scale. When, however, a scale of dividends for $3\frac{1}{2}$ per cent policies is based on an actual interest earning rate of less than 4 per cent, then as long as the same dividend scale is maintained, policy earnings available for dividends tend to diminish with increase in policy duration. This reversal of the traditional trend occurred first on $3\frac{1}{2}$ per cent policies and later on 3 per cent policies.

We in the company with which I am associated approached this situation with great misgivings. We were apprehensive as to how our policyholders would react to such yearly diminution in the amount of dividend apportioned to them. We wondered whether policyholders might erroneously conclude that the general experience of the company was getting worse each year.

But the principle of maintaining equity among policyholders, as well as the bald facts of the situation, finally compelled us to take this unpopular measure. Now that a dividend scale which produces decreasing policy dividends with increasing duration of the policy has become an old story, it is gratifying to be able to report that the reaction of policyholders has not been as unfavorable as we had feared.

Then, as the rate of interest earned fell below the rate assumed for the accumulation of policy reserves, many companies began to be faced with the situation where no dividend at all was being earned on some policies and where, in fact, some policies were actually being carried at a loss to the companies. This situation raised several new questions: Is it consistent with the fundamental principle of participating insurance to declare no dividend at all on such a policy? Where a policy is currently earning a dividend but where, according to the current dividend scale, earnings will become negative some years hence, is it consistent with the principle of equity to ignore such expected future losses and to continue to declare policy dividends equal to current earnings?

The companies have adopted different solutions to this problem. When the company with which I am associated first became confronted with this problem, we adopted the expedient of declaring an arbitrary small minimum dividend for those policies where application of the dividend formula produced either a smaller positive dividend or a negative dividend, and we maintained that practice until it became manifestly inequitable. (There is reason to believe that this is still the practice of some companies under policies which were originally issued on a 3 per cent interest assumption.) Then some years ago we adopted our present practice of declaring a dividend of one dollar per thousand where the formula produces a dividend from seventy-five cents to one dollar, and of declaring no dividend at all where the formula produces a dividend less than seventy-five cents. You will note that this rule enables the company to recover a small but negligible part of the probable future deficits under such a policy.

On the other hand, some companies have attempted an entirely different solution of these problems. They equate the excess, if any, of probable future diminishing earnings available for dividends over probable subsequent increasing deficits into a constant or even an increasing policy dividend. This principle is exceedingly complicated to apply but it has the virtue of being probably the most equitable solution of this problem and, in the long run, the most satisfying to policyholders. Aside from the complication of application, an important objection to this solution is that it immediately results in a large drop in policy dividends, and, if the principle of equity be strictly adhered to, in a greatly enlarged group of policies on which no dividend at all is being declared—a result so drastic that unless rightly timed it is difficult to explain to policyholders.

Reserve Strengthening. When the rate of interest earned on the funds of a company falls substantially below that required to maintain reserves on a large portion of its business, the company is confronted with another serious problem. This situation is definitely an element of weakness. Even though such an element of weakness may be offset many times over by other elements of hidden strength, yet a company in that situation is exposed to the embarrassment of having the element of weakness pointed out by a competitor. It is not surprising, therefore, that in recent years the life insurance companies have strengthened reserves on life insurance policies and annuities originally issued on the higher interest assumptions of the past, assumptions which at that time seemed conservative.

The ten largest companies included in Table I may be used to illustrate the extent to which reserves have been strengthened. Every one of these ten companies has strengthened either life insurance reserves, or annuity reserves, or has established a special reserve for future interest requirements, and some have done all of these things. In 1930, only three of these ten large companies maintained all life insurance reserves on an interest assumption of 3 per cent or less; in 1947, six of them maintained all of such reserves on an interest assumption of 3 per cent or less. On the average, these ten companies maintained life insurance policy reserves on an interest basis of 3 per cent or less on only 56 per cent of their reserves in the year 1930, on 59 per cent of their reserves in 1940, and on 81 per cent of their reserves in 1947. Much the same picture is applicable to annuity reserves.

Such reserve strengthening has not been confined to 3½ per cent policies and other contracts. One of these ten largest companies has set up 2¾ per cent reserves on all of its business originally issued on a 3 per cent basis. Another has set up 2½ per cent reserves on all life insurance policies originally issued on a 3 per cent basis and has set up 2 per cent reserves on all annuities.

The marked tendency during recent years to strengthen reserves is also evidenced by the rate of interest required to maintain all reserves, both insurance and annuity, in these ten large companies. On the average, the rate of interest required to maintain reserves in these ten large companies was 3.23 per cent in 1930, 3.21 per cent in 1940 and only 2.92 per cent in 1947. Note that most of the reserve strengthening has occurred since 1940.

Reserve strengthening such as has taken place during recent years involves the transfer of huge amounts from surplus to reserves. For example, our company had issued all policies prior to January 1, 1935 on the basis of a 3½ per cent interest assumption. The company now holds 3 per cent reserves for all such policies, annuities and settlement options, including a special reserve for interest requirements on probable future settlement options guaranteed on an interest basis exceeding 3 per cent. The amount required so to increase such reserves represented nearly 4 per cent of total liabilities as of December 31, 1945, the date when most such reserve strengthening was effected. Inasmuch as life insurance companies usually maintain a surplus equal to some 4 per cent to 7 per cent of total liabilities, you will appreciate that such a transaction involves the transfer from surplus to liabilities of a very large proportion of the surplus of the company.

Some idea as to amounts involved in a reserve strengthening program consummated by the ten largest companies included in Table I may be had from their published annual statements in those cases where a sum has been set aside in a special reserve; for example, as of December 31, 1947 one had set up $27,000,000 as a "special provision for interest requirements"; another had set up $19,200,000 for "reserve for change in valuation basis on insurance and annuities"; another had set up a "special reserve" of $41,037,565; another had set up $40,000,000 as "additional reserve for prospective policy proceeds."

In his address made December 9, 1948 before the Annual Meeting of the Life Insurance Association of America, Mr. Leroy A. Lincoln, President of the Metropolitan Life Insurance Company, and then President of the Association, throws additional light on the huge sums involved in reserve strengthening. He said:

A factor of much greater importance to the companies and their policyholders has been the sharp decline in the interest rate over the past twenty years—a drop in the rate earned from more than 5 per cent to less than 3 per cent. The resulting decrease in interest made it advisable for many companies to transfer funds from surplus to strengthen their reserves. The effect of such an increase in reserves is illustrated by the fact that if a company's reserves are all based on the assumption of earning $3\frac{1}{2}$ per cent interest and the company has a surplus that amounts to 6 per cent of its reserves, a re-determination of its reserves on a 3 per cent interest basis would entirely eliminate the surplus of the company.

Reserve strengthening on this scale is obviously a matter of major importance. It is a step which a company is likely to take only after prolonged and most serious consideration. It is a conservative measure, because it removes a weakness from the financial structure of the company and it strengthens the capacity of the company to meet the unknown conditions of the future. A part—and in some companies a major part—of the amount taken from surplus to strengthen reserves represented recent non-recurring additions to surplus arising out of investment profits, such as those realized on the sale or call of bonds, produced by the same factor which induced such reserve strengthening, namely, the decline in the interest rate. Nevertheless, for most companies such reserve strengthening is accomplished without undue strain on surplus only by apportioning over a period of years lower policy dividends than could otherwise be apportioned and, therefore, either sacrifices a competitive advantage or incurs a competitive disadvantage in the quest for new business. That reserve strengthening has already been consummated on so vast a scale is evidence of courageous as well as conservative management.

IMPACT ON SETTLEMENT OPTIONS

The interest rate is the all important factor in determining the guarantees under settlement options; for most settlement options, it is the only factor. As a rule, settlement option guarantees are computed without any provision for expense, the assumption being made that expenses, which are not inconsiderable, will be met out of excess interest earnings over and above the rate assumed in the calculation of such guarantees. In those settlement options which involve a life annuity, the assumed mortality rate is also a factor in computing the guarantee; but the mortality factor involved in the calculation of annuity guarantees has almost always, if not always, produced a loss to the companies—a loss which may or may not have been offset by excess interest earnings. It follows, therefore, that in order to avoid a loss a company must earn a higher rate of interest than the rate assumed for the calculation of settlement option guarantees.

The determination of the rate of interest assumed for settlement option guarantees in new policies is fraught with the greatest of difficulties. It involves a forecast of the interest rate over a great many years in the future. Inasmuch as settlement options do not become effective until after the termination of the basic life insurance policy by death, maturity or surrender, it is the interest rate during the subsequent period that must be forecast. If a company be too conservative in such forecast, then it immediately suffers in competition, because liberal settlement option guarantees are now an important factor in competition when so large a part of the new business is sold in terms of income for dependents. At no time in the history of life insurance have life company executives felt so uncertain as to the future of the interest rate as they have felt in recent years.

In New Policies. It is not surprising, then, that the companies have drastically reduced the interest rate assumed for settlement options in new policies. Referring again to the ten largest companies included in Table I, one of the companies did not in 1929 automatically include settlement options in its policies. Of the other nine companies, in 1929 six assumed 3 per cent interest for settlement option guarantees, and three assumed 3½ per cent interest; by contrast, in 1948 seven assumed 2 per cent interest and two assumed 2¼ per cent interest. You will note that there has been a greater reduction in the rate of interest assumed for settlement option guarantees than there has been in the rate of interest assumed for policy reserves and, for the reasons already expressed, that is as it should be.

Thus the companies have reduced settlement option guarantees contained in new policies to the extent called for by recent experience and future prospects. But how does this affect policyholders? We have already seen (Table II) that it now costs 21 per cent more than it did in 1929 to maintain a $1,000 ordinary life policy. But $1,000 of life insurance produces a lower income under a settlement option contained in a 1948 policy than did $1,000 of life insurance under the similar settlement option contained in a 1929 policy.

What has been the increase in the cost of providing a given number of dollars of income? Let me illustrate by the cost of maintaining enough ordinary life insurance issued at age 35 so that if the insured dies during the twentieth policy year when his wife is age 55, she will be guaranteed a monthly income of $100 a month for life with ten years income certain. This is a typical settlement option producing a somewhat smaller income if the insured dies earlier and a somewhat larger income in the event of later death. Using the averages of the ten companies whose experience is included in Table II, in 1929 it would have been necessary to buy a $17,500 policy, the net cost of which for twenty years, according to the 1929 dividend scale, would have been $6,178, or an average of $309 per year. Under a 1948 policy, to provide the same number of dollars of income, the policyholder would have to buy $22,950 of life insurance, the net cost of which for twenty years, according to the 1948 dividend scale, would be $9,823, or an average of $491 per year. In short, the cost of providing such a life income has increased 59 per cent.

This 59 per cent increase in the cost of providing a life income of the same number of dollars is a fair measure of the impact of lower interest earnings on those policyholders who buy life insurance for the income it will produce. Substantially all of this increase in cost is due to lower interest rates. Although there has been a considerable improvement in mortality during this period, the net effect of such improved mortality is quite small; for it operates in the direction of reducing the cost before the death of the insured and then in the direction of increasing the cost after his death because of the greater longevity of the beneficiary as well as of the insured. The 1948 Life Insurance Fact Book, published by the Institute of Life Insurance, shows that expenses over this period had increased by only 3 per cent of the premium and interest income; hence little of this increase in cost is due to higher expense rates.

Nor can we dismiss this 59 per cent increase in the cost of providing the same number of dollars of monthly income with the statement that it is just part and parcel of the general increase in the cost of living and is typical of the increase which has taken place in the general price level. In order to provide the same quantity of food, clothing and shelter that was formerly provided by an income of $100 a month, it is now necessary to provide an income which, when expressed in dollars, is increased in proportion to the increase in the general price level. In other words, the policyholder who wants to insure his wife an income for life sufficient to provide the same quantity of food, clothing and shelter, must now not only provide a larger number of dollars of monthly income—larger in proportion to the increase in the general price level—but each dollar of such monthly income now costs him 59 per cent more than it did twenty years ago. This additional 59 per cent increase in cost is the approximate measure of the added burden on a large and increasing proportion of policyholders due solely to the reduction in the interest rate.

In Old Policies. Settlement options in old policies pose quite a different set of problems. Most of the policies issued during the past forty years or more by the life insurance companies of the United States included at the time of issue settlement option guarantees computed on the basis of interest assumptions which seemed reasonable, even conservative, when they were adopted. Of course, the companies must fulfill such guarantees regardless of whether or not a loss is incurred. Quite obviously a company which is now earning 3 per cent interest on its funds is losing money on settlement options computed on a 3½ per cent basis; it is losing money even on 3 per cent settlement options to the extent of the expense margins which it is failing to recoup out of excess interest earnings and to the extent that the actual death rate under annuity settlement options is lower than expected according to the mortality table at which those options were computed. Reference has already been made to the extensive program of reserve strengthening consummated by the life companies with respect not only to settlement option reserves but also to settlement options which may in the future come into being under policies now in full force. The financial problem arising out of the more liberal settlement options contained in old policies has, of course, become the more serious because of the vastly increased use of settlement options by policyholders and beneficiaries—a part of which increased use is probably due to the liberality of such old settlement options as compared with current returns on conservative investments.

Policy Loan Interest

The reduction in the rate of interest earned by the companies has been reflected in a reduction in the interest rate required on policy loans. Twenty years ago, the typical policy loan interest rate stipulated in new policies was 6 per cent; it is now 5 per cent.

Conclusion

We have seen that the force of the impact of lower interest earnings on the life insurance companies and on policyholders has been indeed severe. We have noted that in falling from 5 per cent earned in 1928 to 2.8 per cent earned by the companies in 1947, the rate of actual interest earnings has fallen below two critical points, namely, 3½ per cent, the rate of interest originally assumed by many companies for the accumulation of policy reserves and then 3 per cent, the minimum rate so assumed prior to a few years ago.

It has been noted how the companies responded to this severe challenge. Policy dividends were promptly and repeatedly reduced. Premium rates were promptly increased for nonparticipating insurance, then premiums for low rate participating policies were increased and more recently high rate participating premiums were increased. The lower rate of interest earnings likewise has been reflected in lower settlement option guarantees and in a lower rate of interest on policy loans. Huge amounts have been transferred from surplus to reserves in order that reserves on old policies as well as on new policies may hereafter be accumulated at a rate of interest more nearly in keeping with current prospects. We have seen, too, that by these measures the companies not only have absorbed the interest losses of the past but also have allocated vast sums for reserve strengthening, without significant reduction in the ratio of surplus to liabilities. The impact of lower interest earnings has borne heavily on policyholders and will continue to do so; for we have seen that it now costs 21 per cent more to maintain a given face amount of ordinary life insurance in force and, in a typical case, 59 per cent more to provide a given number of dollars of life income to the beneficiary.

It is not within the scope of this paper to attempt to predict the future. Nevertheless, it seems to me that something would be lacking if it did not briefly call attention to the possibility that the downward trend in the interest rate has ended, at least for the time being. During the past year and a half, or thereabouts, the rate of interest obtainable on new life company investments has not only stopped falling but has increased a little. Interest obtainable on new investments is for the first time in many years at just about the same rate as is being realized on old investments. If the yield on new investments should continue at about the present rate, then the rate of interest earned on all life company funds should continue at about the present level. There is reason to be hopeful, therefore, that the downward trend in interest rates has at long last come to an end. Although there is as yet no impressive evidence of an upward trend in the rate of interest earnings on life company funds, you may rest assured that if the rate of interest does rise appreciably, the improvement in interest earnings will be promptly passed along to the benefit of policyholders.

CHAPTER II

IMPLICATIONS OF THE GUERTIN LEGISLATION

By Henry H. Jackson, F.S.A., F.C.A.S.*

By Way of Introduction

Authors who set out either to provide what the intelligent man should know about this or that or to produce the intelligent woman's guide to something or other usually come up with a massive tome and can not even be depended upon to stop short of the second volume. But be of good cheer—we shall not attempt an exposition of all that the intelligent student of life insurance should know about the recent Standard Nonforfeiture and Valuation Legislation, conveniently referred to as the Guertin legislation. Instead, we shall try to point out some of the underlying problems with which you must be familiar in order better to understand that legislation. With these problems in mind, the diligent student will take a genuine interest in the solutions offered by recent statutes and may even feel inclined to hazard an educated guess as to where we are to go from here.

To be more specific, we must do a bit of exploring in the realm of assumed yearly rates of mortality, assumed yearly rates of compound interest, and commutation tables, those invaluable tools of the actuary combining both elements. These are usually referred to with that awkwardly obscure word "commutation" deleted. Familiar examples are the Combined Experience Table with Interest at 4 per cent, the American Experience Table with Interest at 3 per cent, the C.S.O. Table with Interest at 2½ per cent. We must glance at the nature and meaning of reserves. We must consider, however cursorily, the guaranteed nonforfeiture or surrender values which form a distinctive part of American life insurance policies. For our purpose, the two terms

---

* Vice President and Actuary, National Life Insurance Company.

may be deemed synonymous, since surrender, whether formal or constructive, produces the nonforfeiture value, whether elective or automatic. The different types of settlement available on surrender, though important, need not concern us in the present broad outline. Comments will be limited almost exclusively to what is not too happily termed ordinary insurance as distinguished from industrial and group, and will refer no more than casually to any collateral benefits so often associated with ordinary contracts.

LIFE INSURANCE IN THE UNITED STATES

It is not necessary to emphasize to you the importance of life insurance as a social institution. We are fortunate enough to live in a country ideally situated, it would appear, for the conduct of that business with the utmost success for all concerned. In the United States we find extending uninterruptedly across a vast continent a single monetary system, a universal language, no tariff barriers, and a popular government dedicated to the principles of private initiative, free enterprise, and the dignity of the individual citizen. Add to this a land of seemingly inexhaustible resources, of unimaginable wealth, and of unparalleled prosperity, whose scores of millions of inhabitants enjoy a standard of living high beyond precedent, and you have a nation where the opportunities for the beneficent and appropriate application of life insurance to the needs of all the people, with a minimum of restrictive supervision and a maximum of ingenious skill, are unmatched anywhere else in the world. How unfortunate it would be if in such a nation, where life insurance is regulated by different and possibly conflicting statutes and supervisory authorities in forty-nine separate jurisdictions, this particular type of public service should be seriously handicapped.

The seriousness of such a handicap because of conflicting legislation is well illustrated by state laws relating to marriage and divorce. Under these laws, Mr. W., divorced, as he supposes, from the first Mrs. W. and living happily with the second Mrs. W., finds himself at a loss to ascertain except through court procedure whether the first Mrs. W. is still his wife to whom he pays a settlement allowance or his divorced wife to whom he pays alimony. Obviously, the position of the (presumed) second Mrs. W. is more embarrassingly ambiguous, the ambiguity extending even to the significance of that initial W, whereas his own status ranges all the way from lawful domestic bliss to bigamy. Worst of all, certain states seem to find it to their advantage to take no steps toward giving us nationwide legislation which is adequate, equitable, and uniform in its provisions relating to marriage and divorce.

The Objectives of Insurance Supervision

Insurance legislation and supervision should be made adequate, equitable, and uniform if the benefits of the institution of life insurance are to be spread as broadly and economically as possible throughout the United States. It is because the Guertin legislation represents an exceedingly important step toward providing just such insurance legislation and supervision that it deserves all the solid study you are capable of bringing to bear on it.

The facts themselves are simple enough. More than ten years ago, at the instance of the President of the National Association of Insurance Commissioners, a committee under Mr. Guertin's chairmanship was instituted to study the need for a new mortality table. It is greatly to the credit of the Association that this progressive step was initiated long before there was any expectation that the Supreme Court would render its celebrated 1944 decision classifying insurance as commerce and therefore, unless it was strictly an intrastate affair, subject, if necessary, to Federal jurisdiction. The first valuable report of the Guertin committee, presented in 1939, expressly recognized that the need for a new mortality table or tables did exist. But it went much further by suggesting that the whole problem of mortality tables is inextricably combined with the related problems of appropriate valuation standards and satisfactory nonforfeiture requirements. The committee was accordingly instructed to continue its investigations. These produced final reports, presented in 1941 and 1942, suggesting the type of standard insurance legislation which has, broadly speaking, been incorporated in state laws and has now become effective.

As a result, ordinary policies issued since January 1, 1948 in the United States are based, with negligible exceptions, on the Commissioners' 1941 Standard Ordinary Mortality Table (C.S.O. for our convenience). A maximum rate of interest is prescribed, but individual companies may adopt any suitable lower interest assumption—that is, the minimum permissive rate is not fixed by statute. The minimum valuation standard which may be legally employed differs somewhat from the measure of solvency previously in use. The measure of minimum nonforfeiture benefits required to be included in current issues is likewise new. This bald statement concerning recent legislation is obviously meaningless unless you have some familiarity with the old pattern. Indeed, it can not yield its full meaning unless you know how the old pattern came into being.

Something About Reserves

If you were asked, "What is the most important single function which a state insurance department should perform?" you would no doubt answer, "It must establish and enforce valuation standards strict enough to insure the solvency of any well-managed company maintaining them." You would be right. And many of you doubtless know the significant historical steps in the establishment of such standards, but a review of some of them might be not unprofitable.

Long before life insurance was commercially practiced in the United States, British actuaries were well aware that if an increasing risk covering a long period is to be paid for throughout that period by a series of level premiums, a substantial portion of the early premiums must be held as a special fund to guarantee the benefits falling due in the later years. Such a fund maintained for a large group of policies has come to be termed the reserve fund, the reserve liability, or simply the reserve.

It is one thing to recognize the necessity for sound reserves on outstanding insurance contracts and quite another to reach general agreement as to the minimum liability that is requisite and as to the appropriate basis for its computation. Any prescribed basis must depend on perfectly definite assumptions concerning future rates of mortality and future rates of interest. That fact alone indicates that the number of defensible bases for determining the reserve on a single group of homogeneous policies is literally infinite. But if a single measure of mortality is employed and a single rate of interest is agreed upon, the reserve bases available thereunder will still be infinite in number. You may use the full net level premium basis, you may strengthen that basis in any way you please—should anyone choose to be so ultraconservative—you may use under a prospective method a gross premium valuation or any modification thereof; or retrospectively you may modify the net level premium basis downward through a full preliminary term valuation assuming term insurance for any prescribed number of early years; or you may use what is commonly called the full preliminary term basis recognizing one year only of term insurance; or you may use any of the recognized modifications of the full preliminary term, or even make any improvement on these modifications which occurs to you. In short, no serious student of life insurance must ever permit himself to forget that there exists no "one and only" correct basis for ascertaining the aggregate reserve on a given group of policies.

But if a valuation is to be any good at all for supervisory purposes, it must be strict enough to give reasonable assurance of continued solvency for the fund in question. Presumably we still have an infinity of appropriate solutions, but this infinity belongs to a more restricted universe than that first mentioned.

The Full Net Level Premium Method

It was not until 1858 that the establishment of the "existing value" of all the policies of any company doing business in the commonwealth of Massachusetts was prescribed by statute. In the following year the Commissioners of Insurance (and without a doubt that means for practical purposes just one man, Elizur Wright) enforced that establishment by prescribing the full net level premium method, a specific table of mortality, and a fixed rate of interest. Their choice was the Combined Experience Table with Interest at 4 per cent. So wise was this choice concerning mortality that the Combined Experience Table might quite well have been retained for another half-century. It was just as appropriate as the so-called American Experience Table (a title not claimed for it by its author) which a little later became its competitor, then won universal recognition in the United States, and has since maintained its rigid supremacy almost to this very day. The 4 per cent rate of interest prescribed was also a wisely conservative assumption in the American 1850's and for more than a whole generation thereafter.

Wright's implementation of the Massachusetts statute seems an excellent solution of the insurance problems confronting him when those problems are fairly considered. Certain British companies had been playing fast and loose with a prospective gross premium valuation method and actually offsetting genuine liabilities with purely fictitious prospective gains. Instead of taking at zero the negative policy reserves which such a process yields in the valuation of recent issues, they deducted these from the positive reserves on older issues, thereby greatly understating the true total liability. It was high time to call a halt on that. Furthermore, in a period when first commissions and initial expenses were low—comparatively speaking, exceedingly low—the Wright method was not seriously burdensome even for young companies, if conservatively managed.

A MORE REALISTIC RESERVE METHOD

But times have changed in nearly a century. It is now generally conceded that in an institution which distributes its benefits as widely as possible over a vast population, initial expenses must be substantial and must include rather handsome first commissions. The net level premium basis of valuation blinks this hard fact, since it compels the initial premium to do the impossible: to meet all first-year claims, to meet all first-year expenses, and to produce a substantial first-year reserve. Any insurance legislation prescribing the unmitigated employment of such a standard is making the establishment of new mutual companies, however well-managed, quite impossible. In recognition of the failure of the net level premium valuation method to meet the actual conditions under which American life insurance is sold, various states have devised as minimum valuation standards numerous modifications of the net level premium method, no one of which has been universally recognized as satisfactory in all the other states. The Guertin Committee, wishing to do a workmanlike job, felt it necessary, therefore, to secure reasonably uniform legislation validating the appropriateness not only of the C.S.O. Table but likewise of some minimum valuation standard applicable thereto. The result is the Commissioners Standard Valuation method. For practical purposes this may be described as a modified preliminary term method very similar to the Illinois Standard which had already gained recognition in a number of important states.

Something About Nonforfeiture Values

If the new legislation was to be adequate, it must tackle another problem only indirectly related to the establishment of a mortality table both modern and conservative and of a valuation standard both sound and practicable. It must seek some sort of consistency in determining the minimum nonforfeiture values available to those throwing up their insurance contracts. This type of legislation is one of the most curious in all the history of insurance supervision. In its inception it was a unique American product. If a man buys a lot for the purpose of building a house, gets an architect to draw his plans, hires a contractor to put in the cellar walls, and then in discouragement gives up the whole business, I am not aware that any legislation would intervene to protect him against undue loss resulting from his infirmity of purpose. Now a life insurance policy may be viewed as being on precisely the same footing as a projected house. The ill-starred builder had contemplated not an investment but a home. Likewise, the applicant for life insurance, properly speaking, is not making an investment. He is buying a service and, as more than one writer on insurance subjects has pointed out, it is a service which he presumably will need all his life. Certainly, a policyholder of 70 whose wife is living has a beneficiary still very much in need of protection when the relative longevity of men and women is properly considered.

Competition among the best insurance companies could be trusted ultimately to compel the equitable treatment of retiring policyholders. But Elizur Wright, the successful sponsor of the first prescribed nonforfeiture provisions, felt that self-regulation within the business would be too slow. Besides, he had a sharp eye on companies other than the best. In the resulting legislation it was no doubt natural that the reserve values already established for an entirely different purpose should be linked with the surrender values to be defined by law.

Reserve values for a group of policies were established to guarantee solvency, although, as previously indicated, there can never be a single divinely appointed sum which alone can represent the "correct" reserve for any particular group. However, an exact sum may readily be computed which does accurately represent the legal reserve according to an established standard. It was perhaps inevitable that once such a recognized basis for the computation of reserves in the aggregate had been established, we should come to *speak* of the reserve per $1,000 as being so much. Then a tiny, facile step might bring us to *think* each individual policy in some miraculous fashion possessed an individual reserve. Actually, the phrase "reserve per $1,000" must logically be interpreted as a short-cut expression referring to that fraction of the total reserve fund on a group of homogeneous policies which each unit of $1,000 of insurance must on the average provide. To me it seems as absurd to refer literally to the reserve of an individual policy as it would be to speak of the *average* age, height, or weight of some designated person at a particular moment of time. However, once the reserve per $1000 is used as a measure, some relation thereto may be set up as a prescribed surrender value. Indeed, it might have been difficult when nonforfeiture laws were first passed to suggest any better measure. Just as soon as the surrender value of a policy was measured by law in terms of the reserve thereon, less a legitimate deduction therefrom, it was again perhaps inevitable that this deduction should be described as a surrender charge, though the terminology has proved both unfortunate and extremely misleading.

Since the old, established companies ordinarily employed the full net level premium valuation method and were forced by circumstances to describe nonforfeiture values in relation to reserve values, it was easy for the unscrupulous to insinuate, and difficult for the policyholder at the moment hard-pressed financially to doubt, that each individual policy had its own individual reserve—very likely the net level premium reserve, absurd as that obviously appears—that this reserve was the true measure of the equity on a policy surrendered in the early years, and that the surrender charge was, in consequence, some sort of penalty imposed as a forfeiture on the poor fellow whose resolution to be thrifty and altruistic had oozed away.

THE NEW STATUTORY MEASURE OF NONFORFEITURE VALUES

The standard nonforfeiture law as proposed by the Guertin Committee and now so widely enacted attempts to get away from the old diversity and from the unfortunate connotations of earlier insurance laws on the subject by omitting in the description of the required minimum nonforfeiture values all reference to any reserve basis whatever. The language falls back, instead, on describing this minimum value in terms of the net value of future insurance benefits under the contract, in accordance with a prescribed standard of measurement, and the present value, according to that same standard, of an annuity (for a term of years or for life as the plan of the particular policy involved may require) of a stated annual amount. Indeed, a true Guertin Committee statute does not even require that the basis of reserve valuation shall be specified in the policy itself, on the sound theory that the measure of liability to be employed is important to the company and to insurance commissioners but meaningless and perhaps confusing to the individual policyholder. This deliberate omission makes possible on contracts issued after 1947 a change in the valuation basis from that originally contemplated, should rather violent future changes in investment conditions, say, make that course seem desirable to a particular company and to the commissioners of all the states in which it operates.

As students of life insurance, you will readily observe that this approach to nonforfeiture values is simply the establishment of a modified gross premium valuation formula whereby the value sought—not now a reserve value but a "take-away value" to be bestowed on a departing policyholder—is the difference between the present value of the future benefits, measured by a perfectly definite formula, less the present value of the future premiums still payable under the contract, where such future premiums have been shorn of part but not all of their loading. Unfortunately, this concept, plain as it appears to the student of life insurance, is not one familiar to the insuring public. In consequence, friendly critics of the new law complain that in the old days the prescribed surrender values may, indeed, have been bad but were at least capable of definition, whereas current surrender values may be good but are hardly possible to define in language comprehensible to policyholders. They add that actuaries in the old days may have had difficulty in convincing the public that nonforfeiture values were fair, but now are utterly unable even to explain to non-actuarial associates in the home office how they are arrived at. There is still hope that before long insurance commissioners will think that simpler terms than those now prescribed by some of them are quite adequate for describing the basis of nonforfeiture benefits and that these improved statements incorporated in future policies will cease to raise any questions at all in the minds of policyholders. Undoubtedly the total separation of nonforfeiture benefits from policy reserves is a happy consummation, not only for the reasons indicated but also for others at least equally important.

Achievements of the New Legislation

This, then, is the achievement of those coöperating to improve the insurance legislation of the United States: A new standard for fixing minimum reserves required by law has been set and is uniformly accepted. A new nonforfeiture standard likewise acceptable in all jurisdictions has been established. These statutes afford, respectively, to all permanent policy owners, adequate protection; to transient purchasers, the guarantee of a suitable settlement on departure. Possibly the most spectacular feat of these new provisions is the setting aside of the antiquated American Experience Table and its replacement by a new measure of mortality far more appropriately representative of current and presumably prospective experience. This feat alone, were it all that had been accomplished, would in itself constitute a minor triumph of legislation.

As a matter of fact, the Guertin legislation includes several other excellent approaches to uniformity. Improved regulations and a new table of mortality for industrial insurance deserve special mention. Group insurance is another beneficiary of the Committee's research. Proper provision for the handling of substandard business has not been overlooked. A minimum basis for the valuation of annuities according to a prescribed annuitant mortality table—an important subject not even glanced at in the old laws of many states—is provided for in the model statute. This is true likewise of those special features frequently incorporated in life contracts which furnish additional benefits in cases of total and permanent disability or of death resulting from accidental means. In short, a full decade devoted to research, public hearings, committee reports, and legislative inquiry has given us insurance legislation adequate, equitable, and uniform to a degree never realized in this country before 1948—a noteworthy achievement indeed.

DESIDERATA BEYOND STATUTORY REQUIREMENTS

But one need hardly hint that reasonable adequacy, equity, and uniformity in statutes alone will not suffice. If insurance companies operating thereunder are to have proper freedom of action in the "practical study and pursuit of perfection" (that is, in affording policyholders the best possible protection at minimum cost), reasonable uniformity of supervision (that is, the application of the rules-of-the-game on the part of the individual insurance commissioners) is likewise important. And when resort to judicial interpretation becomes necessary, reasonable uniformity in the decisions handed down by the courts of the land must again be manifest.

In the administration of laws as complex and technical as those relating to life insurance are bound to be, the utmost that can be hoped for in the way of such uniformity will be approximate only. Some actuaries may feel that the degree of uniformity which they experienced in the consideration of the wording of new contracts submitted to insurance departments in attempted conformity with the spirit and letter of the new laws was at best no more than rough, and that even to call it rough might in certain jurisdictions be to pay it a compliment. The fact that what was believed clear and appropriate had to be supplemented by a rubber stamp in one state, amended by partial deletion in another, and completed through special endorsement elsewhere was both exasperating and disquieting. It is not, however, at all inexplicable. To meet the deadline of January 1, 1948, generally set in legislation, companies and state departments alike were swamped with details, many of them not made familiar by custom. To iron out all the differences of opinion and interpretation in the rush of the closing months was bound to be difficult and certainly proved in some instances impossible. If here and there some grotesque excrescence in a meaningless endorsement on a policy is the worst that has resulted, we may all rest content and look forward to sane reconsideration when there is time for ampler discussion.

THE SITUATION IN 1948

Chaos Is Come Again is the title of one of the rather old but always fascinating novels of Claude Houghton which happened to lie on my desk the other day. In her dusting rounds, our elderly housekeeper, an intelligent Vermonter not very familiar with Shakespeare, noticed the title and thought it so queer as to deserve comment. "That must be wrong," she said. "It ought to be *has* instead of *is.*" (Such dogmatism may remind certain company officials of scraps of phraseology despotically decreed by some state insurance department or other.) But even the man who knows his *Othello* and remembers all the poignancy of that tremendous sentence might, if cynically minded, have exclaimed, "Chaos is come again," when it seemed so uncertain how many of the states would enact the proposed legislation, and how soon, if ever, it could be made uniformly effective. He might have repeated the remark in the heat of the process of obtaining departmental approval of new policy forms. He might even reiterate it today on observing the varied phraseology which almost any company is forced to employ in its new contracts if it operates in dozens of states, or on collating the wording of the contracts of one company with that of another, or, above all, on comparing the premium rates and the nonforfeiture provisions in any fair-sized group of representative companies. Never, I suppose, has the premium structure in such companies revealed wider diversity, and that despite the fact that for ordinary insurance the C.S.O. Table of Mortality is uniformly employed.

This variety in interest assumptions, in loading formulas, in reserve bases, and in nonforfeiture values is to my mind a favorable omen. It means the exploration of new possibilities and the exploiting of new advantages in rendering an old, thoroughly established, and well-nigh indispensable service. "How," one is frequently asked, "will all these changes affect the old policyholder from now on?" Here, at least, we may be sure of the answer: "Not at all." As the student is well aware, the new legislation is not retroactive. The companies are just what they were last December; their objectives are unchanged; the cost of insurance, as in the past, will be determined by those old, inexorable items of mortality, interest, and expense. If, however, the details of conducting the business can be worked out nationwide with less misrepresentation on the part of designing twisters, under state statutes exhibiting fewer conflicts and fewer incongruities, gains to policyholders of the future, no matter when they bought their policies, will be genuine and may well prove substantial.

A Suggested Comparison

You must not think me guilty of trying to magnify the importance of life insurance in saying that in one respect the position today of all Americans interested in that institution (and who is not?) is a bit like that of our citizens shortly after the adoption of the Constitution. If, on some blustery morning while the first Congress of the Federal era was in process of assembling, you could have questioned an elderly native of northern New England concerning his own reactions to the whole complicated new structure, he might have looked thoughtful a minute and then replied quizzically, "Waal, I don't see as haow it's accomplished much in modifyin' the March weather." He could hardly have foreseen, as one zealous contemporary historian hopes he foresees, that our Constitutional Convention, in dealing with the chaos and problems confronting it, was putting on a "great rehearsal" which one day should guide mankind into the successful production of a drama grander yet—the federation of the world.

At any rate, in the far more restricted world of American life insurance, the recent legislation, brought about through the study of vast problems and the coöperation of countless workers, should give both the buyer and the seller of an insurance policy a less chaotic world to live in. If an insurance salesman were to ask me, "What ought I to do about the Guertin legislation?" I should tell him very sincerely, "Forget it." If you, as students of life insurance, ask me the similar question, "What ought we to do about the Guertin legislation?" my only helpful answer must be, "Give your nights and days to the study of the Guertin Committee Report dated June 21, 1939, and yet more nights and days to its final report, including the supplement dated June 8, 1942. Next, consult the statutes enacted as the result of these reports in important representative states. Then, review the current policy forms issued in compliance with those statutes by a few of the excellent companies. Finally, if you are in a very industrious mood, try your own hand at framing the perfect modern life insurance policy."

In conclusion, one ought perhaps to add in the manner of certain novelists who, however, put their disclaimers at the beginning: "If anything I have said this evening bears the slightest resemblance to the ideas and suggestions presented in these reports, these statutes, and these contracts, any similarity to such actual ideas and suggestions is purely coincidental and very likely deplorable."

CHAPTER III

INVESTMENT TRENDS AND PROBLEMS

By James J. O'Leary, Ph.D.*

One of the most significant developments in the American economy since the turn of the century has been the rapid growth of life insurance. The amount of such insurance in force in United States companies rose from $8.6 billion in 1900 to approximately $191 billion at the end of 1947, or an increase of twenty-two times.[1] Along with this expansion of insurance in force there has been an even greater growth in the total assets of United States life insurance companies, from $1.7 billion in 1900 to about $51.7 billion at the end of 1947, or a thirtyfold increase.[2] There is nothing strange about this remarkable record of growth; it is a natural fulfillment of the desire for security on the part of an increasingly large and wealthy American population.

The record of growth in assets of all United States life insurance companies provides a rough measure of the increased importance of life companies in the American capital markets. During the decade 1901-10, the average annual increase in the total of life company assets amounted to $196 million. The average annual increase in the period 1920-29 amounted to over one billion dollars, which was also about the rate of expansion during the depressed 1930's. However, during the period 1940-47 inclusive, the average annual growth in total life insurance assets rose to $2.8 billion. The annual rate of expansion was $2.9 billion in 1943, $3.3 billion in 1944, $3.7 billion in 1945, $3.4 billion in 1946, and $3.5 billion in 1947.

But even these impressive figures do not provide an accurate picture of the total funds life insurance companies have had for investment in recent years. They merely show the increase in

---

* Director of Investment Research, Life Insurance Association of America.
[1] *Life Insurance Fact Book* (1948), p. 11.
[2] Data on life insurance assets in this and the following paragraph are taken from *ibid.*, p. 46.

assets of the companies growing out of the annual excess of income over disbursements; they do not show the additional funds life insurance companies have had available for investment as a result of the "turnover" of their existing holdings. These additional funds have accrued in part as the result of amortization features in, and the maturing of, insurance investments. In the main, however, they have been the product of heavy debt refunding operations which accompanied the steady decline of interest rates from the early 1930's until quite recently.

The firming of interest rates during the past year has sharply reduced the volume of debt refunding, but it has been estimated that during 1948 life insurance companies as a whole will receive something like one billion dollars from mortgagors in the amortization or repayment of mortgages, about $200 million from corporations in the repayment of debt, and approximately $100 million from the Federal Government in the repayment of maturing debt.[3] If we add these figures to the excess of life insurance cash income over disbursements in 1948, expected to be about $3.3 billion, it is clear that the life companies will have something like $4.6 billion to invest this year.

Too much of the current thinking on the investment problems of the life insurance business is based on a mere recital of the facts regarding the growth of assets or funds available for investment. Impressive as these facts may be, the absolute increase of funds flowing into the capital markets via life insurance companies means very little unless it is related to the supply of customary outlets for these funds. This point will be developed more fully later in the discussion.

This lecture is divided into two main parts: (1) a relatively brief discussion of life insurance investment trends since 1940, and (2) a longer discussion of current and prospective investment problems. My views on life insurance investment problems must be regarded as preliminary in nature and in the process of development. The only justification for offering them to you at this time is that they may serve to provoke your own thought. I would also like to make it clear that any ideas I put forward

[3] G. L. Harrison, *Some Observations in Equity Financing*, a speech delivered before the New York Chapter of the American Society of Chartered Life Underwriters, April, 1948.

are solely my own and do not necessarily represent the views of the Life Insurance Association of America or its Investment Research Committee.

INVESTMENT TRENDS SINCE 1940

The War Period. Tracing the investment trends of life insurance companies during 1940-45 is a simple matter; the companies put nearly all of their funds into United States Government bonds, as would be expected in wartime. The aggregate assets of all companies increased by $15.6 billion from the beginning of 1940 to the close of 1945, and their holdings of United States Government securities rose by $15.2 billion during the same period.[4] Thus, the acquisition of Federal securities virtually equalled the increase in total assets of the companies. United States Government securities, which constituted about 18 per cent of the companies' assets at the beginning of 1940, represented about 46 per cent at the close of 1945.

The record for other important assets during 1940-45 shows that real estate mortgages increased from $5.7 billion to $6.6 billion; real estate holdings declined from $2.1 billion to $857 million; holdings of the securities of business and industry rose from about $8.5 billion to $11.1 billion; and policy loans and notes fell from $3.2 billion to slightly less than $2 billion.

The enormous expansion of life insurance holdings of Federal debt during the war has had two consequences of great importance. First, it has been a major factor in the decline of investment earnings of the companies, as we shall see presently, for the 2½ per cent return on long-term government bonds was a lower return than the companies had hitherto been earning on other assets. Secondly, through the tools of public debt management and fiscal and monetary policy the Federal Government is now able to exercise a much stronger direct and indirect influence upon life insurance assets and the return on such assets.

The Postwar Period. The postwar capital requirements of our expanding national economy have reopened investment opportunities in private enterprise for life insurance savings. In sharp

---

[4] Data in this and the following paragraph are taken from the *Life Insurance Fact Book* (1947), p. 49.

contrast to the war period, when as we have seen nearly all life insurance funds were channeled into Federal securities, the years 1946 and 1947 witnessed an expanding flow of such funds into the private sectors of our economy, primarily through corporate securities and mortgage loans.

The figures on life insurance holdings of United States Government bonds are particularly interesting. Largely as the result of Federal borrowing during the Victory Loan Drive in the early part of 1946 before private capital needs appeared in heavy volume, insurance holdings of Federal debt increased from $20.6 billion at the end of 1945 to $21.6 billion at the close of 1946.[5] It is noteworthy, however, that in spite of this absolute increase in life company holdings of Federal debt, the proportion of such debt to total assets declined from 46 per cent at the end of 1945 to 44.9 per cent at the close of 1946. The shift from Federal bonds was more evident in 1947, with an absolute decline in such assets of about $1.4 billion, so that life insurance holdings of Federal debt amounted to 39.3 per cent of aggregate assets at the close of 1947 as compared with 46 per cent at the end of 1945. This shift from Federal debt in 1947 was a perfectly natural development in our competitive economy, reflecting a greatly increased demand for capital funds in the private sectors of our economy. By peacetime standards, life insurance assets are still heavily concentrated in Federal debt, and continued reduction of such holdings is to be expected if the private demand for funds remains strong.

In response to the postwar capital requirements of corporate enterprise, the life insurance companies expanded their investments in corporate securities by about 45 per cent during the two-year period 1946-47.[6] In dollar volume these rose by over $1.9 billion in 1946 and by about $3 billion in 1947. The major part of this expansion is accounted for by an unprecedented rise in holdings of securities of corporations other than railroads and public utilities, although public utility investments by life companies advanced substantially in 1947.

In the mortgage lending field also the years 1946 and 1947 were

[5] Data in this paragraph are taken from *Life Insurance Record for 1947*, a report to the membership of the Life Insurance Association of America by Bruce E. Shepherd, p. 5.
[6] *Ibid.*, p. 6.

characterized by a high level of activity. The 1946 increase of $519 million in life company mortgage loans was the first annual increase of any size since 1942, and it was topped by a 1947 increase of about $1.4 billion.[7] Although direct investment in real estate is a relatively unimportant asset item from the standpoint of size, a great deal of current interest attaches to it because of a developing trend among life companies to acquire real estate for investment purposes. Primarily as a result of substantial investments made during 1947 in housing projects and in certain types of commercial real estate acquired for rental purposes, the total real estate holdings of life companies increased in 1947 for the first time in a decade. The estimated net increase of $90 million in 1947 contrasts with a decrease of $122 million in 1946, and it brought the aggregate amount of real estate owned to about $825 million at the end of 1947.

There is no need to discuss other investment tendencies of minor importance during 1946-47. Let us now turn to some of the investment problems facing the life insurance business which are being discussed currently.

INVESTMENT PROBLEMS

The Equity Capital Problem. A relatively new investment problem facing the life insurance business is whether it is essential, for the smooth functioning of our private enterprise economy, that a larger proportion of policyholders' savings be directed into an equity-type investment, and a smaller proportion into fixed-interest-bearing debt. Many executives in the business, acutely aware of their responsibility that life insurance investment operations be carried on in a manner consistent with the maximum safety of policyholders' reserves, have been concerned with the argument frequently made that a greatly expanded volume of life insurance savings must be invested in an equity form if our national economy is to continue to grow and remain healthy. This argument, which I would like to summarize for your consideration, runs as follows.

It is held that in recent years there has been a persistent tendency for a smaller proportion of personal savings to be invested

[7] *Ibid.,* p. 7.

directly in corporate securities and for a larger proportion to flow into institutions such as mutual savings banks, life insurance companies, savings and loan associations, savings departments of commercial banks, and postal savings departments.[8] The significance of the increased flow of savings into the various institutions, it is argued, lies in the fact that savings through these channels are only available in large measure for investment in debt instruments. Added to this, it is noted that in the past several years there has also been a strong tendency for personal savings to take the very liquid form of cash, demand deposits, time deposits, and Federal securities, amounting to about $172 billion in these forms at the end of 1947. The conclusion reached is that the increased flow of savings through the various institutions which confine their investments largely to debt, plus the tendency for persons to save in a liquid form, goes a long way toward explaining an alleged dearth of equity funds in the capital markets today.

It is argued further that there are two serious disadvantages involved in a continuously heavy reliance on debt in the financial structure of American enterprise. In the first place, our financial practices are such that a substantial amount of equity funds is needed in the capital structure of business to provide a cushion for debt. Therefore, it is pointed out, we face the possible danger that sooner or later an excessively heavy reliance on debt finance will eventually choke off investment and precipitate depression. With business concerns heavily burdened with debt, it will become more difficult for them to borrow money, and savings institutions will find their supply of satisfactory debt instruments dwindling. In this situation, there is a danger that institutional savings will flow only sluggishly into investment, thus exercising a depressing effect on the entire national economy.

Moreover, it is pointed out, there is a second disadvantage to excessive reliance on debt finance in that it introduces a strong element of rigidity into the capital structure of business and makes business concerns vulnerable to cyclical downturns in economic activity. Past experience indicates, it is argued, that

[8] See, for example, *Survey of Current Business,* March, 1948, p. 15; M. W. Reder, *The Theory of Investment and the Stagnation Thesis* (mimeo), pp. 14 and 20.

heavy debt in the capital structure of business sets the stage for a prolonged downward spiral of prices once a deflationary movement gets started. On the other hand, the greater the reliance on equity funds, it is contended, the greater the flexibility of our business system to adjust itself to business fluctuations and the better the chance for economic stability.

Until we have better factual support, it is difficult to appraise the thesis put forward above. The best evidence now available indicates that excessive reliance on debt in the nation's financial structure is not an immediate danger, but could be harmful only eventually. Private debt reduction during the war, lower interest rates, and inflation have created a situation in which it seems likely that our economy can stand a substantial increase of debt. Furthermore, we cannot be sure that the apparent scarcity of equity capital in the financial district is not simply a reflection of increased reliance by corporations on funds internally generated through the retention of earnings and the growth of depreciation accounting. A study by Homer Jones in the spring of 1947 indicated that, based on the relation of debt to equity capital in the late 1920's there was then room for a $30 billion increase of urban mortgage debt, a $65 billion increase of corporate debt, and an $11 billion rise of state and local government debt.[9] Writing in the *Survey of Current Business* for March, 1948, Irwin Friend also concluded that,

It is obvious that there is a danger in too great a dependence upon borrowed capital, but analysis of the present financial structure indicates that the current burden of fixed interest charges is less than in previous periods of high business activity. Thus for corporations as a whole it is estimated that the ratio of interest payments to profits before interest and taxes amounts to 8 per cent at present, compared with 12 per cent in 1941 and 25 per cent in 1929. The total amount of interest-bearing corporate debt outstanding today is somewhat lower than in 1929, and interest rates are much lower, though profits, prices, and national income are much higher.[10]

To a very great extent the cause for the scarcity of equity funds lies in our existing Federal tax system. It is now widely agreed

[9] Homer Jones, "Investment Prospects," *The Journal of Finance*, April, 1947, p. 19.
[10] *Survey of Current Business*, March, 1948, pp. 15-16. For a similar statement, see the *Federal Reserve Bulletin*, March, 1948, p. 270.

that high surtax rates in the upper income brackets, double taxation of corporate income, a comparatively high capital gains tax, and other provisions of our tax system have contributed heavily toward drying up the source of equity funds and killing off the incentive for individuals to make equity investments.

Therefore, the first and most important step which should be taken to release the flow of equity funds is a revision of our tax system designed to encourage equity finance. This means such measures as a substantial reduction in the surtax rates at the higher income levels, a plan for permitting individuals to report their incomes on an average basis over a period of years, elimination of the double taxation of corporate income, a lower capital gains tax, and other similar reforms aimed at increasing the supply of equity funds and encouraging risk-taking by business entrepreneurs.

Regardless of tax reform, which will undoubtedly be limited by the heavy revenue requirements of the Federal Government, there still remains the possible question of whether a gradually increased proportion of institutional savings should be made available in equity form if our private enterprise system is to remain healthy and vigorous.[11] This problem has received increasing recognition in the life insurance business, and the Life Insurance Association of America, through its Investment Research Committee, is sponsoring research on the past flow of savings into investment in an effort to procure information to guide future investment policy.

The Problem of Declining Interest Rates. Other investment problems of the life insurance business are closely related to the one already discussed. The most obvious of these is that of declining rates of return on life insurance investments. The ratio of net investment earnings to mean ledger assets for forty-nine companies holding about 90 per cent of total insurance company assets dropped steadily from 5.03 per cent in 1930 to 2.87 per cent in 1947.[12] As a result, and despite a gradual reduction in the guaranteed interest rate assumed in life insurance contracts, it has become increasingly difficult for companies to earn the

---

[11] See, for example, *Survey of Current Business,* March, 1948, p. 23.
[12] *Life Insurance Record for 1947,* p. 10.

amount of money needed to maintain policy reserves. The record shows that only 63.1 per cent of net investment earnings of the life insurance business was needed to maintain policy reserves in 1930, with a margin of excess earnings equal to 36.9 per cent.[13] In 1946, however, 96.6 per cent of net earnings was needed to maintain policy reserves, leaving an earnings cushion of only 3.4 per cent. And this occurred, as we have noted, in spite of a general reduction by the companies in their guaranteed interest rates.

A great deal has been written about the causes underlying the decline in interest rates. One of the most important has undoubtedly been the heavy pressure of institutional savings on the existing supply of interest-bearing obligations. Perhaps of even greater significance has been Federal monetary and fiscal policy designed to provide an "easy-money" situation. Some relief is provided by the recent rise in rates, which has been occasioned by the heavy postwar demand for capital funds.

Declining interest earnings have had one other serious consequence, in addition to the reduction of guaranteed interest rates. They have led to a significant increase in the net cost of life insurance, estimated to be somewhere between 10 to 30 per cent higher in 1946 than it was in 1930, depending upon the type and plan of policy and the age at issue.[14]

Some Problems Involved in Stock Investments. Faced with declining yields on bonded debt, many life insurance investment officers have been attracted to the preferred stocks of established corporations. Because of the better yield on high-grade preferreds, many companies would probably increase their holdings substantially were it not for the valuation problem. This arises from the fact that life companies in their annual statements to insurance commissioners must carry their preferred stocks at year-end market values. Thus, during a period of declining prices for preferred stocks, companies must take a full write-down on their preferreds, which in turn reduces surplus. Heavy investment in preferreds becomes an impossibility under valuation regulations

[13] *Our National Debt and Life Insurance,* Committee on Public Debt Policy, p. 10.
[14] *Ibid.,* p. 7.

which could lead to the wiping out of surplus in a declining market. The solution to this problem seems to be a valuation method which will smooth out the fluctuations in preferred stock prices over time, and will thus remove the threat to surplus.[15] If this were done, life companies could go forward with providing more equity funds through the purchase of preferred stock.

A much more difficult problem is whether life insurance companies should expand their purchases of common stocks. There has been a great deal of discussion on this subject revealing a wide variety of opinion both in and outside the life insurance business.[16] Several studies have been made which indicate that the average return over a period of years on a group of common stocks selected without hindsight has exceeded the return on high-grade bonds.[17] The main problem in the case of common stocks is again the fact that they must be carried at market value in company statements, and with their strong propensity to fluctuate in value there is the constant danger of heavy writedowns in the value of stocks with consequent reduction in surplus and the threat of technical insolvency. It has frequently been suggested that individual companies can meet this problem by establishing special reserves to take care of market fluctuations in common stock prices, but here also, in the interest of encouraging equity finance, a new method of valuation which would

[15] See, for example, *A Proposed Method for the Valuation of Preferred Stocks Held by Life Insurance Companies,* prepared under the direction of the Life Insurance Investment Research Committee.

[16] For support of stock purchases by life companies, see *TNEC* Monograph 28-A, pp. 33 and 52; S. H. Nerlove, "Should Life Insurance Companies Be Permitted to Buy Common Stocks?", *The Journal of Business of the University of Chicago,* April, 1932, p. 173; B. H. Smith, "Common Stocks for Life Insurance Companies," address at the meeting of the American Life Convention, Oct., 1946, pp. 3-4; Homer Jones, *"The Optimum Rate of Investment,"* a paper delivered at the meeting of the American Economic Association, December 29, 1947, p. 22 (mimeographed copy); R. F. Maine, "Common Stocks as Life Insurance Investments," *Journal of the American Association of University Teachers of Insurance,* March, 1947, p. 50. For opposition to stock purchases, see *TNEC* Monograph 28-A, pp. 3 ff.; T. I. Parkinson, *Address* delivered at a meeting of the New York Metropolitan Department, September 30, 1941; G. L. Harrison, *Some Observations on Equity Financing;* "Life Presidents' Views on Equities Talk by Harrison," *Eastern Underwriter,* April 30, 1948, p. 1.

[17] See the following: *Common Stock Indexes,* Cowles Commission Monograph No. 3; Dwight C. Rose, "A Policyholder's Interest in Equity Investments," *TNEC* Monograph 37-A, pp. 36 ff.; B. H. Smith, "Common Stocks for Life Insurance Companies," pp. 9 ff. and 19-20.

smooth out market fluctuations would be helpful.[18] As a matter of fact, the whole philosophy of valuation of life insurance assets needs to be reconsidered to take account of the fact that the life companies never have had to liquidate their holdings in any volume because almost invariably their current income has been sufficient to meet current obligations. Moreover, with the life insurance business holding a large percentage of corporate securities, mass liquidation of life insurance holdings of these securities would be an impossibility in any event. An added factor in the picture is that the life insurance business now holds some $18 billion of highly liquid government securities.

One last problem, but by no means the least, needs to be mentioned in connection with life company purchases of common stock, namely, the problem of control over corporate affairs inherent in common stocks. There is little doubt that heavy common stock purchases by life companies would eventually place them in a position of control over much business activity and might raise the spectre of anti-trust action. You can understand that this is a matter of real concern both to the life insurance companies and to the state regulatory authorities. The solution here might lie in state laws restricting life insurance companies to a small proportion of any one issue.

Some Problems Involved in Direct Investment in Rental Housing. Life insurance company investments in rental housing projects already completed and now occupied provide housing for 100,000 persons and represent an investment of $138 million.[19] An additional $262 million of insurance investments in rental housing is now under way or planned. There is no denying the great social importance of life insurance investments in rental housing, for they not only aid in meeting the housing shortage, but also contribute to the flow of equity funds in our economy. However, serious problems now militate against such invest-

---

[18] Robert F. Maine suggests the use of special reserves to meet the problem of market fluctuations in common stock prices. See "Common Stocks as Life Insurance Investments," *Journal of the American Association of University Teachers of Insurance,* March, 1947, p. 53. See also, S. H. Nerlove "Should Life Insurance Companies Be Permitted to Buy Common Stocks?", pp. 172-173; B. H. Smith, "Common Stocks for Life Insurance Companies," pp. 20 ff. Smith suggests a 5-year average for the valuation of common stocks.

[19] *Life Insurance News Data,* January 28, 1948.

ments. The basic difficulty arises from the fact that life companies are being squeezed between rising building costs, on the one hand, and comparatively fixed rental fees on the other. Rents on new housing are not, of course, fixed by law, but are governed by the general public's attitude on what constitutes a fair rental charge. Frederick H. Ecker, Chairman of the Board of the Metropolitan Life Insurance Company, recently stated that,

. . . The tremendously increased costs and inability to make firm contracts illustrate the difficulties and, it must be emphasized, represent for the present almost insurmountable hurdles to private enterprise, particularly the investment of fiduciary funds in direct ownership of real estate. The practical result is that until this condition is corrected, the investment of fiduciary funds in housing must be largely restricted to loans secured by insured mortgages or by substantial equity capital.[20]

Another matter which causes grave concern among life officers planning investments in rental housing is the fear of a sudden collapse of the housing market as a result of overbuilding or a general deflationary development in the national economy. In an effort to meet this problem life companies are giving careful attention to the building of a quality of housing which will insure a lasting demand and to provisions for accelerated amortization of the investment. Finally, not the least of the problems involved is that of insurance company control over housing and the public relations difficulties which may arise under that control.

The Purchase of Income-producing Real Estate and Lease-back.
In recent years an increasingly popular investment outlet of life insurance companies has been the purchase of income-producing real estate and its lease-back to the original owners. The property purchased has consisted of warehouses and loft buildings, department stores, industrial plants, hotels, and similar properties. Many of the leases have been for long periods of time and have been on terms that cast doubt on whether these deals can be considered genuine equity investments.

The main problem faced by the life companies, of course, is

[20] *Housing,* an address at the opening general session of the Annual Conference of Mayors, New York City, Feb. 16, 1948, p. 14. See, also, an article by Jean Wilson, *The Journal of Commerce,* March 29, 1948, p. 1.

to take every precaution that the properties purchased give promise of yielding the expected income over the period of the lease. To a considerable extent this has been a matter of restricting such purchase and lease-back arrangements to the highest credit risks and to business firms promising the best chances for continued prosperous existence. Another consideration of prime importance, however, has been careful selection of the type of property purchased. The objective here has been to avoid the purchase of property limited to a single use, as for example a cotton textile plant. Commercial property having a variety of uses has been sought in order to minimize risks.

Other Problems. There are a number of other problems facing life insurance investment officers which are worthy of discussion if time permitted. For one, there is the trend in recent years toward direct placement of loans by life companies. The best information available indicates that at the end of 1946 the life insurance companies held about 2,000 directly purchased issues amounting to approximately $5 billion. This type of purchase directly from the issuers may be distinguished from securities purchased through the regular channels of public distribution. In view of the fact that securities purchased directly from the issuers are not rated or quoted in the market, perhaps the main problem for the insurance business and supervisory authorities arising from the practice is to find a satisfactory method for valuing direct placements in company statements. This question will soon be studied by an all-industry committee on valuation of assets in the insurance business. Some other questions which are being considered by insurance company officers, supervisory authorities, and investment students are: (1) How, if at all, should these loans be restricted in the interest of diversifying risk to the lenders? (2) Do such loans provide insurance companies with greater control over the affairs of borrowers than exists in the case of securities purchased through the regular channels of public distribution? and (3) Does the practice of direct loans place smaller insurance company lenders at a disadvantage with larger companies?

Finally, one of the most difficult problems facing life insurance investment officers today is to keep themselves fully informed on

Federal policy as it affects their operations. As pointed out earlier, in our modern economy with the enormous Federal debt, the United States Treasury and the Federal Reserve Board have great power to influence the yield not only on government bonds but on all securities. Therefore, the investment officers of life companies are faced with the task of understanding the investment implications of current public debt management, fiscal and monetary policy, and if possible anticipating the future direction of such policy. This is no mean job in view of the complex ramifications of such policy.

CHAPTER IV

PRINCIPLES AND PROBLEMS
OF SELECTION
AND UNDERWRITING

By Pearce Shepherd, F.S.A.*

FUNDAMENTAL PRINCIPLES OF UNDERWRITING

Underwriting in its broadest sense includes the determination of premiums, the fixing of contract terms, the sales and service operation for the applicant (field underwriting), and the classification of the risk (home office underwriting).

We are primarily concerned with home office underwriting, that is, the processing of applications in the home office to determine whether or not they should be accepted, and if accepted, on what terms. This process is made necessary by the principle underlying life insurance that every insured should contribute his fair share toward the risk involved. Stated another way, this principle is that only applicants who are exposed to comparable degrees of risk should be placed in the same premium class. The fact that mortality varies with age makes it necessary to have premiums that vary with age for a given plan of insurance; the process of selection and classification of risks is necessary to reflect the fact that individuals of the same age can be classified into groups that will give widely different mortality results. The objective in both cases is equity.

In any group of individuals of the same age, some are on their death beds, some are ailing, some are exposed to greater risks of death because of occupational or other activity, the great majority are "normal" (that is, have had some minor illnesses or have minor physical defects but none that appreciably affect longevity), and some few are free of even the slightest impairment—are superstandard. It is knowledge of the way the various

* Vice President and Associate Actuary, The Prudential Insurance Company of America.

factors influence mortality that enables the underwriter to classify applicants into groups that will give relative mortality rates very close to those that are anticipated. Those subject to a higher than normal mortality are said to be "substandard" or "impaired"—their prospect of longevity is impaired.

If you will picture a frequency distribution, you will have an idea of this classification problem. The range of possible mortality classification—theoretically from zero to infinity—is shown along the base line. The relative number to be found at each classification is shown on the vertical axis. The hump in the frequency curve would center somewhere around a figure representing 100 per cent mortality. It would have a rather short arm on the left-hand side, extending down to perhaps a figure representing 80 per cent mortality, and it would have a long arm extending out to the right, reaching out far enough to include those who are on their death beds. That frequency curve pictures in general how individuals of the same age are distributed with respect to mortality hazards and why it is possible to classify them into groups giving widely different mortality results.

Insurable interest is basic to any discussion of selection and classification of risks. I am going to refer to it in some detail later but for the present we need only to understand that for an insurance contract to be sound, the one who is to benefit from the proceeds must be in such a relationship to the insured that he suffers a pecuniary loss by the death of the insured, which loss is only in part compensated for by the proceeds of the insurance. Any other basis involves an element of gambling.

Given such a sound relationship between the insured and the beneficiary and between the amount of insurance and the finances of the insured, the purpose of selection can be stated in several ways:

1. The standard premiums charged are based on assumptions as to mortality, interest, and expenses. The mortality assumed is based on an experience of insured lives which were selected. (This has been true ever since the earliest days of life insurance.) *Selection at least as effective must be exercised in the future if mortality is to be kept within the mortality provided for in the premiums.* (The fact that mortality has been improving for several years should not be allowed to obscure the importance of this general principle. In the late 1920's insured mortality was

not improving—selection was not yielding as favorable mortality as premiums based on prior experience had assumed. Such a condition may possibly occur again.)

As a corollary it may be stated that selection is not concerned with hazards that are universal because such hazards are reflected in the general mortality level assumed. In a community where everyone has had malaria, little note would be taken of it but the general level of the mortality would be higher than for a healthy community. In a community where malaria is comparatively rare, a history of it in a given individual would set him apart from the normal group.

2. The fact that mortality is improving is not a sound reason to accept at standard rates groups that will definitely give a mortality substantially above the normal even if the addition of these groups would increase the average mortality only slightly. If, for example, mortality has improved so that current experience shows 4 deaths per thousand where 5 deaths per thousand were anticipated in the premiums, it is not sound to include a relatively small group of lives expected to show a mortality of 10 per thousand even if the addition of that group would raise the mortality only to 4.2 per thousand. It would obviously be unfair to increase the cost of insurance for the normal lives by giving some substandard lives standard insurance. *Considerations of equity compel an insurer to continue to select applicants with care even if general mortality is improving.*

3. A company which would accept small known substandard groups at standard rates would be handicapped in comparison with competitors who secure a better mortality because they do not follow this practice. *Considerations of competition make selection a continuing necessity in spite of improving mortality.*

4. The various groups at a particular age that can be identified with respect to mortality—ranging from those who are super-select to those who are on their death beds—may show relative frequencies as indicated in the frequency distribution above described.

As a practical matter the standard class must include a large percentage of the total—otherwise the percentage of substandard policies issued and applications rejected would be very large and dissatisfaction would result. *The large normal group should, therefore, be insured at standard rates.* (This presupposes that the better than normal group is small and not too much better than normal. If the mortality is too much better, other considerations might compel an insurer to charge lower rates. In a tropical country, for example, Europeans and Americans residing in native communities would be subject to a much lower mortality than the "normal" native group and should accordingly be charged lower premiums.)

5. Insurance which is freely offered will attract some individuals who will conceal information that would lead an insurer to reject them or classify them as substandard. Experience indicates that others who may be honest but for reasons best known to themselves seek relatively large amounts of insurance, are likely to give a higher than average mortality. *Selection is necessary to combat "anti-selection"—selection on the part of the applicant who knows or suspects more about his chances of dying than a reasonably prudent insurer could be expected to discover.*

The true purpose of selection is a composite of all these purposes. Briefly stated, it is to determine a premium rate for the risk which is satisfactory both to the insurer and the insured.

UNDERWRITING PROCEDURES AND THE FACTORS INFLUENCING MORTALITY

There has always been some process of securing data for use in selecting and classifying risks. This process has evolved over the years from the practice at one time of having the proposed insured personally appear before the Board of Directors of the insurance organization to the present practice of requiring applications, examinations, and inspection reports. The information sought through these procedures is along lines that will aid in evaluating the various factors which are known to affect mortality.

Eleven of these different factors may be listed briefly at this time. They are:

1. Build, or height and weight and its distribution.

2. Family history, or the background of inherited characteristics.

3. Physical condition, or characteristics such as pulse rate, heart sounds and blood pressure, condition of lungs and other organs.

4. Personal history of illnesses and ailments.

5. Occupational accident and health hazards, and the hazards associated with poor environment which is usually dependent on occupation.

6. Habits with respect to alcohol and drugs.

7. Moral standards.

8. Residence or travel in unhealthy or hazardous areas.

9. Aviation hazards. (These may be connected with occupation, travel, or avocation.)

10. Avocations.

11. Race, nationality groups, immigrants.

Sometimes a twelfth factor, plan of insurance, is listed on the assumption that a desire for low cost protection (term insurance) is unfavorable and a desire for high cost endowment insurance is favorable. It is true that the plan of insurance applied for is one of the things that is considered in evaluating the risk. It is something that, associated with other information, may have an influence on the final decision, but it is not a factor affecting mortality in the same sense that the other eleven are.

We have a considerable store of information about how these factors influence mortality. Some of this comes from general knowledge and observation. Some of it comes from experience in clinical medicine. Some of it comes from statistics accumulated by industrial groups or by government organizations. The most valid source of information is mortality studies of insured lives made by individual companies or by groups of companies combining to pool their experience. There have been a number of such studies and they have been the principal guide to the proper classification of risks. Unfortunately, it has not been possible in recent years to make mortality studies, but the companies may be expected to bring their underwriting information up to date as soon as it is possible to get the help to do it.

PROVISION FOR EXTRA MORTALITY

It is quite obvious that the effect on mortality of some of the factors listed are (1) independent of age (e.g., passenger aviation hazards), (2) temporary and largely independent of age (e.g., the hazards immediately following some acute illnesses), (3) almost entirely independent of age (e.g., some occupational accident hazards), or (4) presumably a function of age (e.g., most physical impairments). At a particular age an extra hazard can be expressed either as n extra deaths per thousand or as m per cent of standard mortality. For all ages or a group of ages one method may be more expressive than the other; each oversimplifies the problem. In practice, the anticipated extra mortality may be indicated in either way with possibly two or three age groups needed for particular impairments, whichever method is used.

If only one of the factors listed in the previous section is significant in a particular case, it makes little difference how the anticipated extra mortality is expressed, but if two or more factors are significant it is necessary to decide how the combination should be stated. There may be two or more items making up the physical condition or personal history factors; in addition, any one of the other factors may be involved. Further, they may all be interrelated, as, for example, in the case of the overweight bartender with high blood pressure who occasionally drinks to excess and who lives in an unsanitary tropical city; or they may be unrelated, as, for example, in the case of the locomotive engineer who a year ago had one kidney removed because of an injury. Any method of classifying risks must solve the problem of assessing as a whole risks that involve two or more factors. This may be left largely to judgment but a systematic method is clearly desirable.

The "numerical rating method" is a systematic plan of rating each of the factors which influence mortality, by a "debit" for those which are unfavorable, and by a "credit" for those which are favorable. It was originally described as follows:

The underlying principle in the numerical method of medical selection rests on the assumption that the average risk accepted by a company has a value of 100 per cent, and that each one of the factors which make up a risk shall be expressed numerically in terms of 100 per cent, and that, by the summation of them, or by some modification of their summation, the value of any risk shall be determined and expressed with relation to that standard. . . . Wherever there is clear evidence that two factors are interdependent so that their addition is not sufficient or is distinctly too large, allowance is made for that interdependence.[1]

[1] Rogers and Hunter: "The Numerical Method of Determining the Value of Risks for Life Insurance," *Transactions, The Actuarial Society of America*, XX, pp. 274-75.

The numerical rating method is the one that is most commonly used and, except for some obvious instances where it does not apply, has advantages over any other methods. It recalls to mind the frequency distribution of risks which was previously mentioned since it is designed to place an individual in his proper position on that frequency distribution with respect to each of the factors affecting mortality.

There was considerable criticism of the numerical rating method when it was first announced but these criticisms disregarded two important points in the original plan. They overlooked the fact that the summation of the risk wasn't necessarily a sum of the individual debits and credits, and that factors which were interdependent called for special consideration.

After the anticipated extra mortality has been expressed—numerically or otherwise—it is necessary to translate that expression into an extra premium or some other means of providing for the extra mortality. There are several ways in which this may be done.

The most common way is to charge an extra premium in addition to the standard rate. Such extra premium may be "flat"—that is, the same at all ages; or it may vary with age. It may be temporary or continuous. The nonforfeiture values may be different from those in standard policies. A method more popular in earlier days than it is now consists in giving a substandard applicant age x a policy at standard rates for age x *plus r*. Another method, also commonly used in the early days and still occasionally applied, is to give the applicant a policy issued at the regular rate of premium but with a "lien" which reduces the death benefit payable. The lien usually reduces over a period of years. Hence, the method is best adapted to extra mortality that presumably disappears after a few years.

A very satisfactory method for a large company treats each substandard class as a special group with respect to premiums, nonforfeiture values and dividends, and thus reflects the actual experience of the group.

In exceptional cases such as one involving an aviation hazard that is difficult to assess to the satisfaction of both insurer and proposed insured, a policy may be issued at regular rates of premium to cover the normal hazards, and coverage for the extra aviation hazard may be excluded. This method is almost entirely limited in application to aviation hazards. It is a device that should not be used too frequently because wherever possible it is desirable to give full coverage at a proper premium.

The underwriting process results in approval of 85 per cent of the applications at standard rates, approval of 10 per cent on some substandard basis, and rejection of 5 per cent. These figures represent the results of a group of ordinary companies as determined by the Institute of Life Insurance and they are fairly typical of results for any ordinary company doing a reasonable substandard business.

SUMMARY OF GENERAL PRINCIPLES

We have covered, up to this point, most of the general principles of life insurance underwriting. These principles may be summarized as follows:

1. The term "underwriting" covers a broad field but our discussion is for the most part concerned with the home office process of selection and classification of risks.

2. The aim of all such processes is fundamentally to attain equity as among applicants.

3. Insurable interest is basic to sound insurance and has been assumed to be cleared before the process of selection and classification is considered.

4. Evaluation of the risk is determined by considering the various factors which affect mortality in the light of all the information available with respect to each factor.

5. The final process *evaluates the risk as a whole* and fixes the terms of the contract to be offered to the insured.

OTHER UNDERWRITING PROBLEMS

A number of features of underwriting which have not thus far been discussed should at least be mentioned briefly so that they will not be passed over completely.

The underwriting of disability benefits issued in connection with life insurance presents some special problems. The most common disability benefit provides for waiver of premium. Some companies still issue an income disability benefit and are confronted with the difficult task of underwriting applicants who are interested in securing that coverage. The underwriting of accidental death benefits has problems of its own.

Non-medical underwriting is simply a problem in economics. At the younger ages and for the smaller amounts of insurance, it is possible to underwrite without a medical examiner's findings because the saving in expenses more than offsets the additional claims that are incurred.

Establishment of limits for the maximum amount that will be issued on any one life or establishment of limits for various underwriting procedures present other types of problems.

Then there are peculiar underwriting problems presented in handling reinstatements and changes. Most of them concern the establishment of standards which will be considered reasonable and adequate.

Up to this point the discussion has been limited to the underwriting of ordinary policies. Underwriting of industrial insurance presents some special problems, mostly because of the small policies involved and the consequent need of less costly underwriting procedures. The matter of agency organization is a consideration in industrial underwriting and it may lead to different problems in smaller companies than are encountered by the larger industrial insurers.

Group insurance is a field of its own. In talking of group insurance today we are talking of more than group *life* insurance. Group insurance, as the term is now used, includes all kinds of sickness and accident, hospitalization and surgical coverages, and even medical reimbursement. The group companies in fact are now underwriting welfare plans.[2]

Most group life insurance is on a one year term basis. The principal characteristics which seem necessary in order that such a coverage can avoid the difficulties that make assessment insurance unsound are:

[2] The principles of group underwriting were covered fully in an address "The Social Responsibility of the Group Insurance Industry" by Edmund B. Whittaker, Vice President in Charge of the Group Insurance Department of The Prudential Insurance Company of America, given at the Fifth New York State Managers and General Agents Conference of The Life Underwriters, Saratoga Springs, February 27, 1948.

(1) The group must be a single cohesive whole, membership in which is based on some strong motive other than that of obtaining insurance, and such that the provision of insurance on a group basis is a natural outgrowth of the relationship of the members of the group to each other.

(2) There should be a steady stream of new entrants to the group, to offset the increasing age of those remaining and thus keep the average cost of the insurance within reasonable limits.

(3) There must be a single administrative organization to act on behalf of the insured group without the insurer having to deal separately with a number of smaller units, thereby avoiding loss of the economies and underwriting safeguards of regular group life insurance.

(4) There must be some mechanism for securing and maintaining the enrollment in the insurance plan of at least 75 per cent of those eligible, thereby avoiding undue adverse selection.

(5) There must be a reasonably simple method by which the policy-holder can collect from the insured members of the group their contributions to the cost.

(6) If at all possible, there should be some party other than the insured member to pay a portion of the premium, thus reducing the cost to the insured member and making the insurance more attractive to him, thereby assuring continued participation in the plan. This is particularly true because the premium for group life term insurance increases with advancing age, and in order to secure and maintain a high percentage of enrollment, the cost to the younger members of the group should be no more than the cost of similar insurance on an individual basis.[3]

RECENT DEVELOPMENTS

With this general background in mind, let us now go on to a discussion of some recent developments and current problems in underwriting, taking each of the principal factors affecting mortality heretofore mentioned. At the outset, however, one point should be made clear. There has been a marked reduction in mortality generally in recent years. This is especially true at the younger ages. Such an improvement in mortality does not make the selection process unnecessary. It is particularly needed to maintain equity among applicants, that being one of the several conceptions of the purpose of selection previously stated.

The evaluation of a risk is generally started with the factor of

[3] Interim Report of Group Insurance Committee, Canadian Association of Actuaries, October 9, 1947.

build. Most of the present build ratings are based on inter-company experience published over thirty years ago. A test of this experience was made in connection with the 1929 Impairment Study. That test indicated that average weights and, more important, the effect of under- and overweights on mortality shown in the earlier study were substantially the same in the later experience. In other words, the same degree of overweight resulted in the same degree of excess mortality that had been found in the earlier study. Therefore, ratings based on this earlier study still seem to be adequate and equitable. There has been an improvement in the standard mortality, of course, but it means that, relatively, overweights are still just as bad as they ever were.

There have been some changes in the importance attached to family history in underwriting. One view of a tuberculous family history is that it indicates a hereditary tendency to this disease and, therefore, is a factor of great importance in underwriting, especially at the younger ages and if the applicant is under-average in weight. More recently the views of underwriters have been that tuberculosis is purely an infectious disease, that there is no real hereditary tendency, and that the factor of weight is not as important as the earlier studies indicated.

There is, therefore, a difference of opinion reflected in the different practices with respect to tuberculous family history today. The life insurance experience seems to support the idea that tuberculous family history is important and underweight is important. The followers of the pure infection approach will need more time to prove that they are correct.

A family history of cardiovascular renal disease may be of some importance in underwriting. Striking cases are encountered where such diseases are very important in causing relatively early deaths in a family. On the other hand, insurance experience has failed to prove statistically that such histories are of much importance. Neither has there been any evidence that a family history of cancer is significant.

Just as there has been some change in tuberculous family history underwriting, so also have there been some changes in the underwriting of applicants with a personal history of tuberculosis. There is some evidence that this is a more serious impairment than the insurance statistics of the past have indicated.

and that greater caution and heavier ratings are necessary. This evidence comes mostly from clinical studies. These studies indicate that overweight is not the safety factor that the insurance experience shows it to be. They indicate that tuberculosis is not entirely a disease of the younger ages, that the death rate increases with age. There is a suspicion that the group classified as tuberculous in earlier experience included some who were not, and diluted the experience of those who were. We believe the tuberculous group we are getting today is different from that which we studied a few years ago.

About a year ago an item appeared in the newspapers concerning the Veterans Administration release of a booklet to its tuberculosis patients, giving them encouragement that the disease could be conquered. The dispatch included some statistics. It said that tuberculosis was causing, on the average, 200 deaths per month in the Veterans Administration hospitals. Later it indicated that the number of such patients in the hospitals as of a certain date was 13,369. This latter figure may not truly represent the population from which the 200 deaths per month arise because many of those who die may be brought into the hospital in advanced stages, but the figures do tend to support the idea that there is a very heavy death rate among those afflicted with tuberculosis.

Although it is customary to speak of curing pulmonary tuberculosis, clinical experience indicates that recurrences are quite common even after a period of years and that there is always a hazard where there has been a personal history of active pulmonary tuberculosis.

A number of insurers have in recent years announced that they are willing to insure diabetics who are well controlled and who show no complicating factors. This step was taken on the basis of clinical experience which showed that a great many diabetics can control their condition and can live reasonably normal lives. It leaves in the uninsurable class a great many diabetics who are not well supervised and who do not take care of themselves. It also leaves in the uninsurable class those diabetics who have evidence of the complications that are known to follow in the wake of this impairment.

Some change has occurred in underwriting practice with respect to gastric and duodenal ulcers. There is more of a tendency to regard a history of ulcers as representing a chronic condition —possibly a little more serious than a bad case of "chronic indigestion," but, nevertheless, of the same general permanent character. In the past there was a tendency to regard such ulcer histories seriously, if recent, but rather lightly after there had been an apparent cure for a short time.

The subject of hypertension or high blood pressure is an important one in underwriting. An extensive inter-company experience published a few years ago threw considerable light on the effect of hypertension on mortality. This and previous studies have led to some tightening up in ratings where hypertension is a factor. One of our difficulties with this impairment is that clinical medicine is learning more about it and some of our applicants for insurance may have learned to control their hypertension within limits. We cannot be sure, therefore, that the applicant who presents himself today with a blood pressure of 140 over 90 is the same kind of applicant with respect to mortality that we insured ten or fifteen years ago.

The use of X-rays and electrocardiograms in life insurance underwriting is a development almost entirely of the last ten or fifteen years. It is a field where there is still a great deal to be learned. We do not know yet how to evaluate some of the features that turn up in electrocardiography. We do know that this instrument enables us to pick out some badly damaged hearts and that certainly where larger amounts of insurance are concerned it is a necessary and valuable test for underwriting.

One point about electrocardiograms should be emphasized particularly. There is a rather general view that a normal electrocardiogram means the heart is normal. That is not true. A heart which has been damaged by rheumatic fever and which has a definite organic murmur as a result of valve damage may show a normal electrocardiogram. Even hearts which have been damaged by coronary artery disease may in time show electrocardiograms without any significant evidence thereof. Valuable as electrocardiograms are, they are not quite as valuable as the layman is inclined to think. They are not the complete answer to underwriting heart cases.

There have been significant developments in occupational

underwriting. As a result of the progress made by industry generally in improving accident and health hazards, some occupations may now be accepted at standard rates that formerly called for substandard ratings. But industry has developed new products and these new products have presented new occupational underwriting problems. The plastics industry is perhaps an outstanding example. We do not know yet how important some of these new occupations are in affecting mortality but we have a great deal of confidence in the ability of industry to minimize them.

Development of atomic energy has presented special difficulty. The secrets of processes at atomic energy plants have been kept from us but through the cooperation of the authorities the insurance companies were able to have two of their experts taken into some of the secrets to the extent that we have developed a system of evaluating the hazards by means of a code applying to an occupation, which code is transmitted to us through the Personnel Division of the Atomic Energy Commission. We thus know how to rate an applicant who is engaged in one of these occupations but we do not know the exact reason that the rating is necessary.

There has been a tendency on the part of some insurers since the war to accept army and navy personnel, even those in submarine service, at standard rates. Some insurers, on the other hand, feel that there is still a definite hazard with respect to submarine service and that those so engaged should not be thrown into the larger navy group, which in general does give a standard mortality in peacetime.

Another tendency has been to offer insurance to persons in military or naval aviation at rates which to some of us do not appear adequate. Experience will soon tell what extra premiums are necessary for these extra hazards.

In the Texas City disaster which occurred a little over two years ago, the employees of the plants which suffered the heaviest casualties were considered engaged in nonhazardous occupations. Nevertheless, they were victims of the disaster which occurred outside of their plant. This case is cited to indicate that there may be occupational hazards outside of those pertaining to the individual's particular duties.

The underwriting of applicants who use alcohol to excess has always been difficult. In recent years we have had the development of Alcoholics Anonymous. It appears to be an improvement over previous ways of trying to help excessive users of alcohol. In underwriting we are inclined to give some favorable consideration to membership in Alcoholics Anonymous but we are not inclined to consider it assurance of a permanent cure. You have probably heard the story of the drunk who encountered a police officer and inquired the way to the headquarters of Alcoholics Anonymous. He was given the proper directions and told: "That is the place you should be going. You should become a member." The drunk replied: "Hic—I'm going down to resign."

Moral hazards also present some difficult underwriting problems. A number of years ago we had bootleggers; then we had racketeers of one kind or another. Their field of operation changes from time to time. Currently, one of their favorite fields is slot machine and pin-ball machine operations. This business is under fire in New York just now. The newspaper accounts indicate that 25 per cent of the people in the pin-ball machine business have criminal records.

There have been some changes with respect to residence or travel in unhealthy or hazardous areas as a factor affecting mortality. Control of tropical diseases has improved. The mere fact that an individual can be brought home by air very rapidly somewhat minimizes the hazard. Air conditioning may help to keep tropical residents happier as well as healthier. The experience in tropical areas during the war where conditions were at all under control lends some support to the idea that the hazards of tropical residence are not as great as they were a number of years ago.

There have, of course, been developments with respect to aviation underwriting because this is a rapidly moving industry. Pilots of domestic scheduled airlines are generally insured at extra premiums of $2.50 or $3.00 a thousand today, whereas a few years ago these extra premiums were $25.00, if coverage was offered at all. This reduction in rate naturally reflects the great improvement in safety that has taken place in scheduled airline transportation. Extra premiums have been established for a number of the other aviation occupations which are low compared to those of a few short years ago. These are based on less certain experience and it remains to be seen whether the phases of aviation to which they pertain are as safe as the premiums indicate.

Aviation is, of course, also an avocation and there it presents aviation's most difficult underwriting problem because the proposed insured himself knows so much more about what he intends and expects to do than the underwriter can find out. A great deal of the hazard is within his control. That is why in these cases an aviation exclusion clause is sometimes the best way of granting insurance at a satisfactory premium.

There are hazards connected with avocations other than aviation but in general they are not important in underwriting. The fact that there are such hazards was forcefully brought home to my company not long ago when we paid $200,000 on a claim on a young man who lost his life in a skiing accident.

Nationality groups sometimes present special underwriting problems. A new arrival from a foreign country is something of an uncertain quantity simply because it is so easy for him to conceal part of his past. In recent years those who have come to this country as a result of unrest and war in their homeland have presented even more difficult problems because we not only have not known much about their past, but we have realized that they would have some difficult economic and personal problems in getting adjusted to their new surroundings. Caution has been exercised in these cases by requiring them to be in this country for a certain length of time and to be quite well established economically as well as socially.

Racial background is also sometimes a factor in underwriting. A number of United States and Canadian companies operate in the Hawaiian Islands. As you know, the population of the Islands is made up of a number of racial groups. Those of Japanese extraction are numerically the greatest but there are other Oriental and mixed groups. The population mortality in the Oriental countries, and the early experience on similar lives insured in the United States and the Hawaiian Islands, indicated that an extra mortality should be anticipated. Underwriting rules of twenty years ago, therefore, generally classified the majority of persons of Oriental or mixed blood as substandard risks. The highest grade were considered standard. Over a period of years the group acceptable at standard rates has been enlarged as there has been some accumulating evidence of an improvement in population mortality and an improvement in insured mortality. These improvements seemed extensive enough so that something over two years ago underwriting rules for the Islands and Continental United States and Canada were rather generally changed to consider practically all Oriental lives on the same basis as Caucasian lives. This applies to those who have been born in the Islands or who have been there for a number of years. There still seems to be evidence that those who were brought up in the Orient may be subject to some extra mortality, probably because the native diet habits which they continue are not entirely adequate.

In this country we have a further problem with respect to the underwriting of colored risks. Population statistics show that the colored race is subject to a much higher mortality, particularly at the younger ages, than the Caucasian race. The problem is whether it is possible to pick out from this big population group any part which may be subject to a mortality comparable to that of Caucasian lives.

If you will picture in your mind two frequency curves, each similar to that previously described, one centering around 100 per cent mortality and the other with its peak around 140 per cent mortality, you will have a picture of this problem. The distribution centering around 100 per cent mortality represents the way Caucasian lives are distributed with respect to mortality. The distribution centering around 140 per cent represents the way the colored lives are distributed with respect to mortality.

It appears reasonable to assume, therefore, that there may be some small part of the colored race that is subject to a mortality no greater than a part of the Caucasian race that falls within standard limits. The great majority, however, are in a group that gives a substandard mortality.

INSURABLE INTEREST AND FINANCES

Insurable interest is basic to a consideration of the risk, but underwriting with respect to finances of the applicant is important and should be mentioned particularly because it constitutes a field in which there is often a difference of opinion between the home office underwriter and the agent. In fact, it is frequently quite difficult for the home office underwriter to convince an agent that a man who is willing to purchase a large policy and pay the premium may not be safely insurable.

Insurable interest may be defined as the right to collect insurance benefits on the death of a person to compensate for other and greater benefits that would have been received if the person had lived. Unless the beneficiary stands to lose rather than gain by the death of the insured, an insurance contract is without adequate insurable interest, and insurance without insurable interest is a "mere wager" in law and is prohibited.

In property insurance, such as fire and marine, the contract provides indemnification for loss or damage which may be easily and definitely measured in terms of money, and the claim cannot exceed the value of the property lost. The amount of the loss is not so easily measurable in life insurance and the amount payable on the death of the insured is always the full amount provided by the policy—unless the contract is voided as a "mere wager." It is up to the underwriter to evaluate the probable loss to the beneficiary because he cannot plead excessive insurance or lack of insurable interest as reasons for not paying the claim in full. He must look beyond the purely legal aspects of insurable interest; what may be legal may not be insurable. Legally a man has an unlimited insurable interest in his own life but an underwriter would consider as speculative $100,000 of insurance on an applicant earning only $3,000 a year. The relation which insurance should bear to finances is, therefore, an extension of insurable interest because there should be a proper relation between the amount of insurance and the probable loss. The problem can be summed up in the statement that "life insurance is essentially a contract of indemnity based on insurable interest at date of issue and . . . therefore the aggregate insurance granted should be limited to some function of the financial loss which would be caused by untimely death."[4]

In financial underwriting we are most frequently concerned

[4] J. M. Laird, "Over-Insurance," in *Transactions, The Actuarial Society of America*, XXXI, pp. 82-83.

with valuing earned income. Dr. Huebner has done a great deal to determine the value of insurance that is reasonable with respect to earned income. Our problem currently in this field is the matter of what income we should use as a base. Do we use gross income or do we use income after taxes? Neither base is entirely satisfactory when we are dealing with large amounts. Arbitrary rules are out of place. The situation calls for a fine exercise of judgment on the part of the underwriter to determine what is reasonable under all the circumstances presented in an individual case.

The valuation of an applicant's income from a business presents further problems. Again the underwriter must depend on his judgment as to what is reasonable.

Corporations frequently insure a key man. The commonly accepted rule is that a key man should be insurable for five times his annual salary. On the other hand, we encounter many cases where we are quite willing to go much higher than the five-times rule would permit. Frequently the key man is given bonuses or rights to buy stock at advantageous prices or is otherwise compensated in such a way that his present salary does not measure his value to the company or his value for insurance purposes.

The practice of making deferred compensation agreements with valued employees is a recent development that has some underwriting aspects. It is very difficult sometimes to determine whether or not speculation is involved when a large amount of insurance is required on this basis.

Insurance is sometimes applied for to protect a creditor. Such a use may be quite reasonable if the repayment of the loan depends on the special ability of the insured. On the other hand, underwriters are not inclined to consider a man eligible for insurance just because he is in debt. One sales idea currently advanced is based on the fact that banks will lend money at low interest rates and the interest may be a deductible item in computing personal income tax. Such a plan involves the insured applying for a very large amount of insurance and borrowing a sum equal to all or substantially all of the premiums to pay for it. The insurance less the indebtedness gives him the net protection he desires. Underwriters in general do not look with favor on the large amount of insurance called for under such a plan.

Insurance which is based on investment income is difficult to evaluate. If the insurance is sold, as is frequently the situation, to take care of estate taxes, there are sometimes difficult questions in determining how much is reasonable. The answer may depend on a very thorough analysis of all the circumstances relating to an estate and its owner. A plan of selling insurance was recently advocated on the basis that a man should invest part of his capital in insurance to produce more estate dollars. Most underwriters would doubtless look with skepticism on any such proposal.

We frequently have to underwrite insurance where there is no direct income. Children for the most part fall in this category. They do not present an underwriting problem, however, because usually the amounts are very modest and it is a well-accepted idea that a child's insurance program should be begun early.

Married women frequently have no income but may apply for insurance. Amounts must usually be modest before an underwriter will look upon them with favor. Furthermore, he wants to be sure that the breadwinner of the family is insured first. In fact, the primary consideration in underwriting married women and children is that the father be insured to a reasonably adequate extent, then possibly the mother for a small amount, and then the children.

Financial underwriting has for about twenty years been recognized as very important but it was not generally so considered during most of the 1920's. Mortality on persons insured then for large amounts was very high, especially during depression years, and led to excessive losses. In most recent years financial underwriting has been on a sound basis and the experience on policies issued for large amounts has been comparable to that for all amounts. This, of course, reflects more than just an improvement in financial underwriting. Electrocardiograms, X-rays and more exacting medical requirements have had a part in improving this mortality.

Conclusion

An item in one of the insurance papers not long ago interested me. It recorded a debate held at the Chartered Insurance Insti-

tute in London. The topic of the debate concerned the proposition "That underwriters are born and not made." The vote after
the debate was 37 in favor of the motion "that underwriters are
born and not made." The vote against the motion was 43. The
article then concluded:

> If there were a debate in the United States as to whether under-
> writers are born or are manufactured, the majority vote would be that
> able risk passers become such through long experience and study which
> generate judgment and that few have what might be called a flair for
> the work. Of course, there are some on this side of the water who are
> marvels in snap judgment, just as one sees many sitting at desks at
> Lloyd's, London, ready to accept a risk apparently without more than
> a few moments of hesitation, but the average American home office
> underwriter is a man who does it the hard way—background, remem-
> brance of situations, knowledge of the world of industry, intensive
> study of the risk, fire department and engineering considerations and
> knowing a lot about the agency or the brokerage office which places
> the business.[5]

Of course, the writer of that article had in mind underwriting
of types of risks other than just life insurance itself, but the point
is that underwriting—the selection and classification of risks
which takes place at the home office—is both a science and an art.
It is based on scientific principles, and it requires considerable
experience, skill, and judgment. It is one of the most interesting
aspects of life insurance operations. It is vital to the welfare and
standing of the company. It must be sound and progressive to
keep up the morale of the company's field force, and it is constantly bringing the underwriter into contact with the public
that the insurance companies serve. Home office underwriting
plays an important part in proper relations between the public,
the company's field force and the administration of the company.

[5] *Eastern Underwriter*, February 13, 1948, p. 21.

CHAPTER V

REINSURANCE OF LIFE RISKS

By Walter O. Menge, F.S.A.*

To introduce the subject of life reinsurance, let us consider the situation of a newly-organized life insurance company which has just completed the sale of its stock—let's say 10,000 shares, with par value $10 per share. This was sold, we will assume, at a price of $20 per share, thus creating a fund of $200,000. Of this $200,000, one-half (or $100,000) is represented by capital stock, and this amount must be maintained intact if the company is to avoid insolvency. The other half (or $100,000), which is referred to as surplus, may be used to defray extra expenses required to build up the company in its early years and to pay death losses if the company should experience an unusually heavy mortality which is not covered by the mortality margins in the premiums which it receives. During the first few years of its existence the company will not have a large income from other sources, so that the $100,000 of initial surplus represents practically all of the funds available to pay any excess losses.

An agent of this newly organized company has just sent in an application for a $100,000 life insurance policy. It is apparent that, if the company were to issue a policy for the entire amount of this application and the insured should die during the first year, the company would be required to pay $100,000 to the beneficiary and the entire surplus of the company would be wiped out. Common sense dictates that this procedure is unsound. Carrying all of one's eggs in one basket is just as foolish today as it was when Cervantes wrote *Don Quixote*. It would seem prudent for this company to limit its issue in this and similar cases to a nominal amount, say $2,500. If the company refused to issue a $100,000 policy in this instance, however, its decision would have an adverse effect on the agent, who would soon dis-

* Vice President, Lincoln National Life Insurance Company.

68

cover that the business which was refused by his company had been issued by another company through another agent. To protect his interest, the agent would be tempted to broker this excess business to other companies, even though that procedure might involve a somewhat lower commission, such as is customary with respect to business of this type. Furthermore, the absence of credit toward special prizes and bonuses on such business might soon tempt him to join some other company which would be in a position to give him complete service in this type of situation.

Reinsurance facilities offer a solution to this dilemma. Through the medium of a reinsurance arrangement it becomes possible for the company to issue the entire $100,000 on its own policy form through its agent and at the same time retain only a small amount at its own risk. Reinsurance affords a convenient and inexpensive method through which a company may render an adequate and efficient service to its agency forces, without subjecting itself to the danger of excessive mortality losses which might arise out of a maldistribution of its policies with respect to amount.

With this introduction let us progress to a more detailed analysis of reinsurance as it is practised today in the life insurance business. The term "reinsurance" relates to an arrangement under which one insurance company, known as the "reinsurer" or "reinsurance company," undertakes to reimburse another insurance company, known as the "ceding" or "original" company, for all or a specified portion of the loss which may be incurred under a particular life insurance policy or policies. As may be seen from the illustration previously cited, reinsurance is ceded from the original company to the reinsurer whenever the former desires to issue a life insurance policy covering a risk that it is unwilling to carry itself.

RETENTION LIMITS

Sound management principles would indicate that it is prudent for a life insurance company to avoid wide variations in surplus earnings from year to year. Such variations in earnings might arise out of the occurrence of a few death claims on policies of disproportionately large amounts. Consequently, it is common practice for a life insurance company to establish a schedule of maximum amounts, called retention limits, which it will retain at its own risk on individual lives that fall into various categories. By the adoption of a suitably chosen schedule of retention limits, the company attempts to keep fluctuations in the cost of death claims from year to year within reasonable bounds and thereby avoids wide fluctuations in mortality costs which would influence surplus earnings adversely.

In times of relatively low interest earnings, such as companies are now experiencing, consistent mortality savings are of major importance to a life insurance company. Consequently, it is to a company's best interest to fix its retention schedule at as high a level as it deems safe and prudent, in order to retain for its own account a substantial share of its business.

It is not the purpose of this paper to enter into a technical discussion of the method of determining a proper schedule of retention limits. On a purely theoretical basis this constitutes an interesting problem in the theory of probability. The factors which must be taken into consideration include, among others, the statistical distribution of the number of policies issued at each amount level, the distribution of attained ages, and the amounts of surplus funds available for the purpose of meeting adverse mortality. The problem of retention limits is complicated —unusually so—and in the author's opinion has not been solved on a theoretical basis to the complete satisfaction of most actuaries.

From a practical point of view, however, we can draw some general conclusions. If only a few policies are being issued in excess of a certain size, it is apparent that little is to be gained by retaining the excess amounts. On the other hand, much is to be gained by avoiding the violent mortality fluctuations which may arise out of deaths among these large policies. The retention limit should also bear a reasonable relation to the total expected mortality of the company. If a company's total expected mortality for the year is only $50,000, for example, it would not seem wise to retain $10,000 on any one life, inasmuch as one maximum claim would affect the mortality ratio by as much as 20 per cent and erase a considerable part of the potential mortality margin.

The amount of surplus which a company has available to meet adverse mortality is also an important factor in the determination of its retention schedule. A company with a large amount of free surplus is obviously in position to establish a higher schedule than another company with a comparable distribution of business but with a thinner surplus margin.

The position of the small company, particularly one recently organized, with respect to retention limits is somewhat different from that of the older well-established companies. The total expected mortality of such a company in its formative years is relatively small, and a single claim for an amount four or five times its average size policy would make a considerable difference in its mortality savings. On the other hand, such a company usually has a large surplus in proportion to its liabilities. In such instances it is not unusual for the company to fix a relatively high retention schedule in proportion to the amount of its business in force, in order to retain at its own risk as large a proportion of its business as possible. The decision should depend, in part at least, upon the prospects of the company for future growth, but this is usually uncertain to some extent, and in the final analysis the aggressiveness and courage of the management carries a great deal of weight. (I have heard it said that the retention limit should be the maximum amount of a death claim which the physique of the president of the company can stand when he discovers such a claim in the mail on a rainy Monday morning.)

The number of large policies issued at the extreme limits of insurable ages, that is, on juvenile and elderly applicants, is relatively small. Furthermore, at these extremities of age the mortality rate is higher and it can be demonstrated that the probability of a wide mortality fluctuation is larger at these ages. For these reasons it is common practice among companies to have lower retention limits at the extreme lower and upper ages of issue. This is also true with respect to substandard risks, where the retention limits generally decrease with the degree of impairment of the risk.

Occasionally a company will establish a lower limit of retention for a special class of applicants, such as, for example, those presenting aviation hazards. This is usually the result of either an adverse experience with this particular class of applicants or a feeling on the part of the management that current competitive rates may prove inadequate. Another example of this type is a group, such as those with diabetes, where available information as to the proper mortality class is particularly meager. As a third example, a company will retain less than its established limit of retention, or perhaps nothing at all on a particular case, because of a feeling that the underwriting information is not complete.

Retention limits vary considerably among companies, depending upon the temper of management. This is true even among companies of approximately the same size and financial status. Some companies with relatively high limits for standard business do not retain substandard business, presumably because they feel that the volume of such business will not support the expense of training and maintaining the highly specialized medical and underwriting staffs which are so important in a proper selection of this business. Smaller companies refrain from substandard business because they feel that their small volume of such business is insufficient to give them a stable mortality experience. As might be expected, companies doing a reinsurance business are specialists in the substandard field.

From the foregoing, it becomes apparent that the business received by a reinsurance company will generally fall into two classes: (a) excess cases, that is, reinsurance on lives where the amount applied for is in excess of the ceding company's established limit for the class of risk involved, and (b) special cases, where for one reason or another the ceding company retains nothing or only a part of its usual retention.

Unless the reinsurer is receiving a large volume of reinsurance from a number of companies with relatively small limits of retention, the first class of excess business consists primarily of cases where the total amount applied for and in force on the life in all companies is relatively large. The mortality experienced on this class during the last depression was materially higher than average, although more recent experience on these cases has been somewhat contradictory. It remains to be seen whether the additional X-ray and electrocardiographic requirements usually imposed by the companies on these "jumbo" cases will prove effective in keeping the mortality on this class of business down during periods of economic recession. Excess business is, however, usually of high average size, an important factor in keeping the unit expenses of the reinsurer at a minimum, and this low expense rate offsets, to some extent at least, the increased mortality cost of this type of business.

The second class of reinsured cases is usually free of the "jumbo" risk problem inherent in the first class. Nevertheless, as might be expected from the fact that the ceding company retains little or nothing on each case, standard business in this class is likely to be of borderline quality. Also, a large portion of this class consists of substandard risks, upon which the mortality fluctuations may be relatively large. The average size of the case is smaller than that of the first class, and the unit expenses of the reinsurer are higher for this reason and also because the business is more difficult to underwrite.

REINSURANCE PROCEDURE

Reinsurance contracts are of two general types providing, respectively, for facultative submission of individual cases to the reinsurer for approval or for automatic reinsurance. Under a facultative arrangement the ceding company offers to the reinsurance company such cases as it desires to reinsure. The reinsurer does the underwriting and is free to accept or reject each case as it sees fit. Under this procedure the ceding company sends copies of its application, medical examination, and other pertinent papers to the reinsurance company and then awaits the latter's decision before issuing its policy. Many companies prefer to place their reinsurance in this manner, inasmuch as it gives them an opportunity to obtain the reinsurer's underwriting opinion before the policy is released. Frequently the reinsurance company may receive several applications for reinsurance on the same life from different companies, and for this reason it may have more complete underwriting information than any single ceding company. Inasmuch as reinsurance decisions are usually transmitted by telegraph, there is only a short delay involved in handling reinsurance on this basis.

From the viewpoint of the reinsurer, the receipt of reinsurance on a facultative basis gives it an opportunity to apply its usual underwriting rules. Furthermore, in cases involving large amounts of coverage from several clients, the reinsurer has the opportunity to limit the facultative business which it approves to the maximum which it can handle. In this connection, it should be borne in mind that a company doing a reinsurance business finds it necessary to retrocede business in excess of its own retention to other companies.

Under an automatic arrangement the ceding company agrees to reinsure with the reinsurance company all cases accepted by it for amounts in excess of its usual retention limit and the reinsurance company is bound to accept all such excess up to a predetermined maximum. Under this arrangement the ceding company is enabled to issue its policy without delay and without securing the prior approval of the reinsurance company. Notification of automatic reinsurance is sent to the reinsurer by mail within a specified period after the ceding company issues its policy. By agreeing to accept all business ceded to it automatically, the reinsurer is relying on the underwriting judgment of the ceding company and is bound to accept the case even though it may not agree with the underwriting action. It is protected by the requirement that the ceding company retain at its own risk its full retention limit for the class of business, standard or substandard, that is involved. In actual practice, when any question of insurability exists, the ceding company usually does not use its automatic facilities, but instead secures independent underwriting opinion by submitting the case to the reinsurer on a facultative basis.

When the original company's limit of retention is relatively small, automatic contracts usually provide for amounts of standard reinsurance up to four times the limit of retention of the ceding company. Inasmuch as the reinsurance company may receive automatic cessions on the same life from several ceding companies, the reinsurance company protects itself by making a contract, known as a retrocession contract, for placing any excess reinsurance automatically in another company or companies. Because the amount of automatic reinsurance on a life received by the reinsurer may get out of bounds, the reinsurance contract generally restricts automatic cessions to those cases where the amount in force and contemplated in all companies does not total more than a specified amount, commonly $500,000 at the usual insurance ages. Automatic reinsurance facilities make it possible for the original company to issue policies promptly and thus give efficient service to its field force on applications of large amounts. Because the original company is bound to cede reinsurance automatically, it is usual for an automatic arrangement to provide reinsurance coverage even though death of the policyholder should occur before the reinsurer has been notified that reinsurance has been ceded. This fact is particularly important in cases where the company issues to the applicant for insurance a so-called "binding receipt," under which the insurance becomes effective immediately upon completion of all the required application forms and the payment of the premium, provided the applicant is found to be insurable under the company's rules and limits.

REINSURANCE PLANS

There are two general plans for life reinsurance which are currently in common use, namely, "risk-premium" reinsurance, usually called "yearly renewable term," and "coinsurance."

Under the risk-premium method of reinsurance the ceding company purchases from the reinsurer during each policy year an amount of reinsurance coverage equal to the "net amount at risk" applicable to the portion of the original policy which is reinsured. The "net amount at risk" is the technical name for the excess of the amount of death benefit provided by the policy over the terminal reserve thereon for the current policy year. Since the terminal reserve on most plans of insurance increases from year to year with the duration of the policy, the net amount at risk under the original policy decreases from year to year. Inasmuch as the amount of reinsurance coverage is a predetermined proportion of the net amount at risk under the original policy, it also decreases with duration. As the alternate name implies, the risk-premium method provides for yearly renewable term reinsurance which is renewed from year to year by the payment of reinsurance premiums annually for the entire period during which the reinsurance coverage remains in force, even though the original policy may be issued on a limited payment plan.

Inasmuch as the ceding company pays reinsurance premiums sufficient to cover only the mortality risk, the risk-premium method enables the ceding company to build up the reserves on the reinsured portion of the policy. As might be expected, this consideration appeals to smaller companies particularly, in that they are able to gain the prestige of increased assets and to retain the excess interest earned on these assets. Furthermore, when a reinsured policy terminates, the original company receives the benefit of any difference between the reserve on the policy and the value of any nonforfeiture benefit which it may grant.

The risk-premium method is convenient from the viewpoint of office procedure. In practice, as each case is ceded it is customary to compute a reinsurance schedule, showing respectively the net amounts at risk to be reinsured and the corresponding premiums for each policy year for five years initially, and to compute extensions of this schedule for further periods of five years as occasion arises. If the original policy is changed to extended insurance or reduced paid-up insurance in accordance with its terms, the reinsurance schedule is amended to conform to the revised net amounts at risk. No accounting is necessary for commissions or dividends paid, and terminations are handled easily because no adjustments are necessary for cash values or reserves.

Premium rates charged for risk-premium reinsurance have been reduced materially within recent years. The reinsurance rates currently used by a typical reinsurance company for standard business, for policy years after the first, are equal to the net mortality rates shown by the CSO Mortality Table for attained ages above 30. Slight loadings are added at younger ages. Substandard rates are usually multiples of standard, increased slightly for the additional expense of handling substandard business. First year rates are usually one-half of the corresponding renewal rates.

An alternative general plan used for life reinsurance is coinsurance. This plan parallels the arrangement under which fire and marine risks are coinsured. Under this method the ceding company pays the reinsurer a proportional part of the premiums collected from the insured, and in return the reinsurer guarantees to reimburse the ceding company for the proportional part of the benefits provided by the policy, including nonforfeiture values, policy dividends, and death claim payments. The reinsurer also reimburses the ceding company for a proportional part of the commissions, premium taxes, and other direct expenses, and occasionally, in totally reinsured cases, grants expense allowances for such items as medical examination and inspection fees. The reinsurer also accumulates the required reserves for the reinsured portion of the policy.

Coinsurance is quite common for reinsurance of participating policies, and for this class of business the reinsurer reimburses the ceding company for its full portion of dividends paid to the policyholder, irrespective of the level which such dividend payments may take. In determining its schedule of dividends, the ceding company takes into account only the surplus contributions of the business which it retains, and the reinsurer is required to match this schedule with respect to reinsured business.

The coinsurance plan is also used for non-participating policies, particularly in those situations where there is a severe strain on the original company's surplus in the first policy year. For example, where the original company pays relatively high first year commissions or where it issues policies requiring full net level reserves, the premium received by the original company during the first policy year is usually not sufficient to avoid a surplus loss. In such instances coinsurance relieves the original company of the surplus strain occasioned by the reinsured portion of the policy.

A variation of the usual coinsurance arrangement, referred to as "modified coinsurance," is one under which the ceding company retains possession of the full reserve under the reinsured policy. In remitting premiums under modified coinsurance, the ceding company deducts from the usual coinsurance premium each year an amount which, if invested at a specified interest rate, will be sufficient to accumulate the addition to the terminal reserve for that year on the reinsured policy. In any settlement which is made between the ceding company and the reinsurer, adjustments are made for the fact that the full reserve on the reinsured policy has been retained in the possession of the ceding company. In settling a death claim, for example, the reinsurer pays to the ceding company only the difference between the gross amount at risk and the terminal reserve, both computed on the reinsured portion of the policy. If the policy is surrendered for its cash value, the original company pays the cash value to the insured and remits to the reinsurer the difference between the reserve in its possession and the cash value on the reinsured portion, thus putting both companies in the same position as under regular coinsurance.

Quite frequently, however, the modified coinsurance plan is arranged so as to ignore terminal reserves and to make adjustments for changes in mean reserves on all reinsured policies simultaneously in one transaction at the end of each calendar year. This latter arrangement extremely simplifies the necessary computations, not only in connection with premium payments, but also with respect to death claims, surrender payments, etc. Transactions within each calendar year are handled in the same manner as under regular coinsurance. The adjustment on the basis of mean reserves at the end of the calendar year usually results in the return at that time of a substantial sum of money to the ceding company, and the investment of these funds may be delayed with a consequent loss of interest. This disadvantage is frequently overcome by a special arrangement providing for a monthly return of approximate amounts with an adjustment at the year-end for any overpayment or underpayment of reserves.

Modified coinsurance has been used successfully for many years by European reinsurance companies for reinsurance of foreign business. Its popularity in Europe is probably due to the fact that it minimizes, to a considerable degree, the problems of foreign exchange. Within recent years it has gained some popularity in the United States also.

Reinsurance of disability benefits, which are frequently incorporated in life insurance policies by means of a rider, is on a coinsurance basis, even though yearly renewable term reinsurance may be used for the life portion of the policy. Reinsurance coverage is identical with that afforded by the original rider, and the reinsurance premiums are those charged by the ceding company less allowances for agents' commissions. Disability reinsurance is usually accepted by a reinsurer only in connection with life reinsurance, because of the relatively small premium involved and the complicated nature of the benefit.

With respect to reinsurance of additional accidental death

benefits, however, it is customary for special reinsurance rates to be charged on an annual basis for the duration of the benefit, even though the original policy may become paid-up at an earlier date. Because of the small premiums charged in relation to possible liability, many companies prefer not to retain any of this benefit, and reinsure all that they issue. Reinsurance companies usually accept such reinsurance without a corresponding amount of life reinsurance. For convenience, cessions of additional accidental death benefits without life reinsurance are handled automatically by means of cession cards giving details of the reinsurance, without the usual forwarding of copies of the application and other underwriting information. This short cut in clerical procedure is desirable because of the relatively low premiums involved.

General Reinsurance Provisions

The general rules governing the reinsurance relations between the ceding company and the reinsurer are incorporated in a master reinsurance contract, sometimes called a reinsurance "treaty." Such contracts are usually unlimited as to duration, but provide for discontinuance with respect to the submission of new cases at any time following proper notice by either party. Because it is practically impossible to cover in the master contract all contingencies that may arise, reinsurance relationships depend to a considerable extent upon the good faith and mutual confidence of the two companies. In event of dispute, the reinsurance contract usually provides for arbitration by suitably chosen arbitrators, and both sides agree to abide by the decision. It is extremely rare for this method of settling differences of opinion to be invoked, inasmuch as it is usually possible for the two companies to agree upon a fair and equitable settlement.

As evidence of the basis of good faith and mutual confidence between the two parties to the master reinsurance contract, it is usually provided that, if nonpayment of premiums within the time specified or failure to comply with any terms of the contract is shown to be unintentional and as the result of misunderstanding or oversight upon the part of either party, the agreement is not considered abrogated thereby but both parties are to be restored to the position they would have occupied had no oversight or misunderstanding occurred.

Reinsurance on individual lives is evidenced by a short cession form which merely recites the necessary details with respect to the case. This form is completed in duplicate by the ceding company and sent to the reinsuring company for verification, following which the original is executed and returned to the ceding company for its files.

In order to keep accounting expenses at a minimum, reinsurance contracts provide for payment of reinsurance premiums by the ceding company annually at the beginning of each policy year, irrespective of the mode of premium payments under the original policy. In general, the first year reinsurance premium is not paid until after the original policy has been placed and the first premium received from the insured. The renewal reinsurance premiums are payable in the month following that in which the policy anniversary falls, all payments of reinsurance premiums due in the same calendar month being handled in one transaction. In the event of termination of the original policy within a policy year, the unearned portion of the reinsurance premium is refunded to the ceding company.

In general, master reinsurance contracts provide that neither the ceding company nor the reinsurer has the right to terminate the reinsurance coverage as long as the original policy remains in force and the reinsurance premiums are paid when due. One exception to this rule, customarily provided by risk-premium contracts, is that the ceding company may increase its established retention limits and make the new limits retroactive with respect to existing business in force by adjusting all of its outstanding reinsurance to conform to the new limits. Such increases in retention result in the cancellation or "recapture" by the ceding company of blocks of existing reinsurance. In order to avoid selection against the reinsurer in such instances, it is usual to permit recaptures only on standard cases where the ceding company originally retained its full retention limit. Also, because of the reinsurer's initial expenses in underwriting, the initial cost of setting up records, and the lower first year rates, recapture is generally restricted to those cases which have been in force for five years or more. It is usual to permit recapture only with respect to risk-premium reinsurance, and not with respect to coinsurance, because of the commission and expense allowances involved in this latter plan.

A company, which originally retains some insurance on a life at its own risk and simultaneously or later reinsures additional amounts, usually desires to maintain its own retention on the life, even though the total amount of insurance be reduced by lapse, surrender, or decrease. Consequently, the master reinsurance contract usually provides that any reductions in total amount be first applied to reduce the outstanding reinsurance, even though the reinsurance pertains to an original policy other than the one which is currently affected. Occasionally, however, it is provided that the reinsurance pertains only to a particular original policy and no adjustments in reinsurance coverage are made unless this policy is changed in status.

In settling death claims, the master reinsurance contract usually permits the ceding company to pay the amount of the claim to the beneficiary without prior consultation with the reinsurer. But whenever there is a question as to the validity of the claim, it is common practice for the ceding company to communicate with the reinsurer before making any admission of liability. If a questionable claim is settled by the ceding company through compromise by the payment of a reduced amount, the saving is shared proportionately by the ceding company and the reinsurer; furthermore, any expenses incurred in defending or litigating a claim are shared in the same manner.

The payment of a death claim in an amount different from that provided by the face of the policy may also occur when the age of the insured is misstated. If a misstatement of age is discovered, the amount of reinsurance is increased or decreased, as the case may be, in proportion to the change in the amount of the original policy. Where risk-premium reinsurance is involved, the entire schedule of amounts of coverage and reinsurance premiums is recomputed on the basis of the revised amounts of reinsurance at the correct age, and retroactive adjustments are made in the reinsurance premiums.

A third problem in settling reinsurance claims arises when death occurs during the suicide period of the original policy. In this event the liability of the original company under the policy is limited to a return of premiums. Under these circumstances the reinsurer refunds to the ceding company its proportional share of the policy premiums which are paid in settlement decreased by the terminal reserve.

When fraud is discovered during the contestable period of the original policy and the policy is cancelled by a refund of premiums to the insured, an adjustment is made which leaves the original company in the same position as if the policy had not been issued. It is customary for the reinsurer to reimburse the original company for its proportional share of any expenses incurred in taking up the policy.

The type of reinsurance which has been discussed herein is commonly called "indemnity" reinsurance, under which the obligation of the reinsurer is solely to the ceding company. In actual practice, the insured usually has no knowledge of the existence of reinsurance on his life, inasmuch as the only policy he receives is that of the original company for the full amount of insurance which is granted. The reinsurance is a confidential arrangement between the two companies, and no legal relationship exists between the policyholder and the reinsurer. The liability of the reinsurer is to the ceding company and not to the policyholder on whose life the reinsurance is based. The funds paid by the reinsurer to the ceding company in settlement of a claim become a part of, and are merged with, the general funds of that company and are not segregated for the purpose of paying the specific claim to the beneficiary under the policy.

No attempt has been made to cover in this paper a type of reinsurance called "en bloc" or "assumption" reinsurance, under which the reinsurance company assumes all the rights, privileges, and obligations of the original company, such as occurs through voluntary or involuntary sale of all or a portion of the outstanding business of a company.

Reinsurance Situation Today

Prior to World War I, the bulk of the life insurance business in the United States was carried on by German companies. The outbreak of war in 1917 interfered with the ability of these companies to accept new reinsurance, and the resulting vacuum was filled by the entrance into the field of several companies domiciled in the United States and Canada, which have continued since that time to fill the reinsurance needs of companies on this continent. There is one life insurance company in the United States which accepts reinsurance only. Also, there are several "reinsurance pools" made up of small groups of companies which exchange reinsurance among themselves. The bulk of the life reinsurance in the United States, however, has been transacted for the past thirty years by several direct-writing companies which have established special reinsurance departments.

The Spectator Company reports a total of $3,250,000,000 of ordinary life reinsurance ceded by United States companies and in force at the end of 1948 in the United States and Canada. This is about 2.4 per cent of the total ordinary business in force in these companies.

In conclusion, may I say that the position of reinsurers in the life insurance business is unique. The reinsurance aspects of their business bring them into contact with experienced insurance executives, and they have an important influence on many facets of the business, notwithstanding their lack of direct contact with the original policyholders. By accepting unusual classes of risks on which no one company can be expected to receive a sufficient number of applications to give a broad exposure, they expand the range of insurability for the American public. In assisting companies to give complete underwriting service, reinsurers assist their clients in maintaining loyal and satisfied agency forces, which is beneficial to the institution of life insurance as a whole.

CHAPTER VI

SIGNIFICANT ANNUITY DEVELOPMENTS

By Ray D. Murphy, F.S.A.*

HISTORICAL BACKGROUND

In approaching for the first time in these lectures some of the modern developments under annuities issued by life insurance companies, it may be of interest to recall that in dealing with annuities we are touching upon an old subject which has quite a fascinating history. The history of the development of annuity benefits from the Middle Ages to our own day mirrors some of the changes in religious tenets, in methods of national finance, and in economic conditions wrought by the industrial revolution. And lastly, annuity benefits have a prominent place in the compulsory social schemes which have been inaugurated by governments.

To illustrate briefly some points in this history, it may be remarked that the prohibition as early as the twelfth century against charging interest on loans of money did not do away with the need for capital nor the willingness of the borrower to pay back more than the loan for the use of capital. Neither was imagination deadened by the edict. Consequently, a solution was found in the granting of annuities as compensation for the receipt of capital sums. In fact, the Church itself found it convenient to raise capital by that device.

Developments such as these may well have suggested the raising of money for war purposes through the sale of annuities by national treasuries, as was first done by Holland and England in the sixteenth and seventeenth centuries. As we trace down this history, including the unsuccessful issue of annuity contracts by the British government in the early nineteenth century as a means of refinancing the national debt, we see the first evidences

* Executive Vice-President and Actuary, The Equitable Life Assurance Society of the United States.

84

of the problems involved in the sound handling of annuity contracts.

At first little was known of the mysteries of mortality rates and their influence on the proper pricing of annuities. In some of the early experiments even age was disregarded. Mortality tables when first used in England were woefully inadequate for the purpose. Apparently the first quarter of the nineteenth century had passed before much recognition was given in England to the difference in longevity between males and females. Furthermore, governments have been slow to recognize the losses involved in their annuity operations even when they have been pointed out. In these and in other ways many warnings may be seen of the losses which may be incurred in the issuance of annuities unless the issuer is cognizant of all the problems which the self-selection of purchasers presents, and promptly responds to changes in conditions.

In the United States the common use of annuities as provision for old age arrived relatively late. When the first investigation of annuitants' mortality led to the formulation of McClintock's Annuity Tables, which involved the experience of fifteen American companies up to 1892, about three-fourths of the lives on which the data were based represented contracts issued in Europe by a few of those companies. It is evident therefore that the purchase of annuities in the United States was as yet quite unpopular. There should be little wonder at this. Capital development in the relatively young republic offered the thrifty an attractive means of saving. Perhaps the speculative instinct was also strong, encouraged by developing manufactures, mining, and agriculture. In comparison the assured returns under annuity contracts may have looked unattractive. But beyond that, our social habits were different. Family life was stronger and more stable and many were the households, both in the country and in the cities, that housed three generations. Provision for old age was still primarily a family obligation owed by the younger to the older.

Recent Growth of Annuity Contracts

Shortly after the first World War the sale of annuity contracts by life insurance companies began an upward movement which has brought annuities to a position of prominence never before attained. That this growth of annuity obligations has been much more rapid than the growth of life insurance obligations is shown by the combined figures for fifteen prominent companies. In 1920 the proportion of their policy reserves held for annuity benefits was only a little over 2 per cent, whereas by 1945 it exceeded 22 per cent. A corresponding increase was reflected in the premium income of these companies.

In examining such premium income two important observations may be made. At the depth of the depression of the 1930's the sale of annuities took an enormous upward bound, especially in the field of single premium contracts. The confidence of investors in the securities of private corporations had been rudely shaken. In contrast, such investors were obviously impressed with the inherent stability of the life insurance companies to which their record of weathering wars, epidemics, and now a disastrous blow to the country's economy bore emphatic testimony. An assured return on an investor's capital and the elimination of investment risk took on a unique attraction. The first year premium income for newly issued annuity contracts jumped, for a short interval, to something like fifty to sixty times what it had been in 1920. While the tide then receded somewhat, it probably can be assumed that annuities acquired an emphasis in the public mind which has been of a lasting character.

The second observation relates to deferred annuities through which younger and middle-aged persons can lay aside regular sums annually to provide ultimate annuity benefits when they reach retirement age. Such contracts found little sale in the early years of this century. An examination of the renewal premium income of the companies for such contracts indicates, however, that from about 1920 on the volume of such contracts grew rapidly. This plan of regular annual savings for old age during one's productive period has now received wide acceptance but the form of contract by which it is done frequently combines annuity benefits with some insurance benefit. As the premiums for such a combination of benefits are not split for the separate benefits and are reported as insurance rather than annuity premiums, because of insurance laws and regulations, it is not possible to gather information through regular company statements concerning the total amount of money which is currently being devoted to the creation of the annuity benefits.

In this connection it is appropriate to point out that practically any form of life insurance policy, other than term insurance, may be turned into an annuity benefit. The popularity which sprang up in the 1920's for these deferred annuities, under which annuity income was to commence at any one of a series of ages at the option of the annuitant, through the application of the cash value to buy an annuity on a fixed mortality and interest basis, introduced the thought that a person insured under a life insurance policy might wish to do the same thing with his cash value when he should decide to retire. Hence there was introduced a corresponding provision in many life insurance policies. This made it possible for a man to plan his affairs so that his family might be protected by a substantial amount of insurance on his life during his working years and at an older age he could decide whether to continue this insurance or whether to turn the remaining savings represented by the cash value of this insurance into a guaranteed income for his own old age. In some instances the basis was guaranteed even for turning the cash value into a joint and survivor annuity, presumably for himself and his wife. Altogether, the introduction of guaranteed annuity benefits to be acquired through surrendering the cash value of life insurance made the planning of insurance programs much more flexible and at the same time emphasized the importance to the insurance buyer of skilled planning by life underwriters.

So far we have dealt with annuity benefits arising from individual contracts issued by life insurance companies. Within the last twenty years, however, the old age benefits, put into effect through group annuity contracts issued by the companies, bid fair to take the predominant part in the annuity picture. Undertaken first in response to the needs of large employers for the sound financing of pension plans for employees, they furnish old age protection to that large body of employees who would not ordinarily buy deferred annuity contracts themselves. By the end of 1948, it is estimated there were 2,175,000 people for whom such benefits are being purchased or who are currently in receipt of income from them under contracts issued by United

States companies.[1] As a matter of comparison, it is also estimated that 1,195,000 individual annuity contracts of all kinds were in force in such companies,[2] although, as already pointed out, a very large number of insurance contracts in force are also designed to provide terminal annuity benefits if desired.

The introduction of group annuity contracts served the needs of the employers of large numbers of employees, and made it possible for them to handle their pension plans under expert guidance and with a guarantee of the benefits purchased at a very low rate of expense in proportion to the amount of premiums involved. In general, however, the hand tailoring of each such contract with all the variations in benefits desired was not a practicable step for small employers. At the same time, small employers in many instances have desired to adopt some similarly guaranteed plan and to rid themselves of the vagaries of chance concerning the survival of retired employees, which survival may be subject to more serious fluctuations than in the case of the large employer. The small employer also realizes the uncertainties of any pension plan unless he makes advance provision for it on some guaranteed basis. As a means of filling this need, life underwriters adapted individual contracts to what are commonly known as pension trusts. The employer appoints trustees to whom he turns over adequate sums to meet the premiums of these individual contracts which may be deferred annuities or a combination of insurance and annuity benefits. The trustees in general have the responsibility of ownership of the contracts prior to retirement of each employee and of carrying out the administrative obligations of the trust as they may affect the exercise of rights embraced in the contracts.

There are many complicated problems in these employer-employee contracts arising from federal tax laws and regulations but that is a subject outside the scope of this paper. Details of such contractual plans have also been affected by the old age benefits under the Old Age and Survivors Insurance provisions of the Social Security law, the benefits under which are heavily weighted in favor of the lower income groups compared with the employee taxes exacted. If we consider the O.A.S.I. benefits as

[1] *1949 Life Insurance Fact Book,* The Institute of Life Insurance, p. 25.
[2] *Ibid.*

essentially a provision for minimum subsistence, we may point out that the employer plans dealt with by life insurance companies are designed to increase the total old age benefits to a level which will provide a reasonably comfortable maintenance through old age.

The important influences upon employer plans of this nature would not be completely enumerated without reference to the very recent stress which has been placed upon so-called employee welfare plans in collective bargaining between unions and employers. These union sponsored welfare plans may in some instances be first directed toward group accident and health insurance or group life insurance, but there are growing indications that pension plans are of increasing interest to the unions. It may therefore come about that the character of pension plans, including group annuity and pension trust contracts, will be influenced to a greater extent than in the past by the points of view developed within organized labor. It may be hoped that employers' interest and cooperation, not only in inaugurating such plans but in wishing to do their part toward their successful administration, will not be lost whatever the developments may be.

The Character of Current Annuity Contracts

It would be well now to review the various types of annuity contracts which are commonly available today for purchase from life insurance companies. Not every company sells annuities, nor does every company which sells annuities sell every kind mentioned here.

I. Individual Contracts

These contracts may be participating or nonparticipating. Many companies, although mutual in corporate structure, issue nonparticipating immediate annuities.

Immediate Annuities

(a) **Life Annuity:** A contract, purchased by a single premium, guaranteeing payments of fixed amounts at fixed intervals after purchase, as a rule annually, semiannually, quarterly, or monthly, during the remaining lifetime of the annuitant.

(b) **Refund Annuity:** A contract similar to a life annuity, but with the additional provision that if the annuitant dies before receiving an aggregate of fixed payments equal to the single premium paid, annuity payments will be continued to a beneficiary until such aggregate sum has been paid.

(c) **Cash Refund Annuity:** A contract similar to a refund annuity except that if at the death of the annuitant the aggregate of fixed payments made is less than the single premium paid, the difference will be paid immediately instead of through a continuance of the periodic payments.

(d) **Joint and Survivor Annuity:** A contract similar to a life annuity except that payments continue as long as either of two persons is alive. Variations may be made whereby the income is reduced by some proportion to the survivor after the first death. Also, theoretically, more than two lives may be involved and some refund feature may be added, but such variations are not commonly encountered.

Deferred Annuities

(a) **Single Premium Deferred Annuity:** A contract, purchased by a single premium, under which payments of a fixed amount at fixed intervals commence only after a period of deferment. If the annuitant dies before payments commence, there usually is a death benefit having a value not greater than the single premium paid for the contract, or the reserve at the time of death if larger. There also may or may not be some kind of refund feature where the annuitant dies after annuity payments have begun. The time at which annuity payments are to begin is specified in the contract but the annuitant is frequently furnished with an option to elect after issue the start of income at any one of a range of ages.

(b) **Annual Premium Deferred Annuity:** A contract, purchased by annual (or semiannual, quarterly, or monthly) premiums under which payments of a fixed amount at fixed intervals commence only after a period of deferment. The common form of this contract includes a benefit, in event of death during the deferred period, equal to the gross premiums paid, or the reserve if greater, thereby minimizing the importance of the mortality rate during that period. Commonly also the annuitant has a range of ages at any one of which he may later elect to have income commence. The amount of income is determined by applying the reserve at that time to purchase an immediate annuity on a guaranteed mortality and interest basis at net rates. The annuity is commonly of the kind which has a guarantee that payments will be made, even if the annuitant does not survive, for a certain number of years. There may also be given a choice of a life annuity with all payments dependent upon the annuitant's survival.

Deferred annuities of types most commonly issued, with a death benefit during the deferred period, have cash values available as alternatives to income benefits at maturity as well as during the deferred period. It is theoretically possible to issue a deferred annuity having no benefit payable at the death of the annuitant, thus increasing the income per dollar of premium to the annuitant if he does survive the deferred period; but so few people wish to hazard paying premiums with a chance of receiving no benefit that it might be difficult to find a company which maintains such a contract.[3]

II. Group Annuity Contracts

These contracts are commonly found in any one of three forms to be described later. They are participating in character. Pension credits for future service are covered from year to year as they accrue, and the sums required may be paid by the employer alone or jointly by the employer and employees. Any contributions by employees are normally based upon their compensation. At the inception of the contract, premiums may be paid in a single sum or in installments to cover the pension credits due to the service of employees prior to that time. Such premiums are paid by the employer, even if the contract is otherwise contributory, as a matter of practical necessity in view of their large amounts.

---

[3] The survivorship annuity, under which income is payable to B if and when he survives A, is not included in the description of annuities, as it has the nature of an insurance rather than an annuity contract despite its name. It is also seldom called for because of the chance that there will be no benefit payable.

Such back service, however, may or may not be included under the contract. Employees are commonly brought into the plan after being in the employer's service for a minimum period.

In the contract a normal retirement age is defined as of which the normal pension benefit per dollar of premium paid at each age of any employee may be determined. The contract may also provide, however, that the employer may require the insurance company to commence annuity payments earlier or later than the normal retirement age for any individual employee. In that event the contract indicates how the amount of the annuity payments will be changed so that the value of such payments will remain the actuarial equivalent of the payments based on the normal retirement age, although in some cases annuity payments are not increased by deferred retirement, the employer receiving credit in his costs for the financial effect of deferment.

The contract will further provide the conditions, usually based on the individual's age or service, under which pension credits already paid for definitely vest in the employee so that if he leaves his employment he retains the future benefit of such credits. Prior to meeting such conditions the withdrawing employee normally has the right to withdraw only the sum of his own contributions, or such contributions accumulated at a low rate of interest. If an employee leaves after his credits are vested and he insists on withdrawing his own contributions in cash, he must normally give up the credits purchased by the employer's contributions. This practice serves to encourage the preservation of pension provisions. The employer receives proper credit for forfeited accruals and the company is able to avoid the difficult and economically indefensible task of trying to administer very small pension accruals, as many of them would be, on persons whose subsequent whereabouts would be impossible to trace in many cases.

If an employee dies before pension age, a death benefit equal to his own contributions becomes payable, with or without interest. It is not usual for a death benefit to arise from the employer's contributions because to include such a benefit would materially increase the cost of pensions, which are bound to be expensive even without such a benefit. Death benefits are normally supplied through group life insurance. Returns at the time of death or withdrawal under the group annuity contract are designed to assure the employee that he will under no circumstances forfeit his own contributions.

The forms of group annuity contract currently being issued can be placed in the following general categories: the unit annuity plan, the money purchase plan, and the deposit administration plan.

Unit Annuity Plan

Under this plan, which is the most used of the three, the amount of pension credit payable at normal retirement age for each year of service is fixed by formula related to each individual's compensation. The total premiums paid each year are not of any pre-determined amount but depend upon the individual ages and pension credits in accordance with a schedule included in the contract. Since the employee's contributions, if any, are fixed by his compensation irrespective of his age, the employer's payments are the balance necessary to produce the proper total premiums. It is important to note that each employee is thus guaranteed every year that his pension accrual for that year has become a definite obligation of the insurance company.

In the contract the insurance company usually guarantees for a period of five years the schedule of premiums showing how much must be paid for each dollar of benefit at each employee age. After that the company may alter the rate basis for the purchase of further pension accruals.

If under this plan provision is made for additional payment of premiums for the past service of employees as of the inception of the contract, the usual type of pension benefit providing credits for all years of service can be secured on a completely guaranteed basis for the employees, subject only to the fact that future additional pension credits will depend upon the continued payment of premiums.

Money Purchase Plan

Under this plan, instead of having fixed benefits in terms of service and compensation and then determining the premiums required to provide these benefits, the premiums are first fixed, usually as a percentage of compensation, and the benefit for each employee is then determined, depending upon how much pension the premiums will buy, based on the employees' respective ages when each premium is paid. Thus, for example, if employer and employee each puts in 5 per cent of the employee's compensation, the pension benefit purchased during each year of service will depend upon the employee's age during that year. As it is evident that during the time when an employee is young each dollar of premium will buy a greater benefit payable at retirement than it will when he is in middle life or older, the pension benefits under this plan will be more favorable to those who enter it at lower ages as compared with those who enter in middle life, than would result under a unit annuity plan. However, as each premium is paid, the employee's corresponding pension accrual becomes definitely guaranteed by the insurance company.

In many instances these future service credits are supplemented through purchase by the employer of credits for past service. Such credits often are based on a formula similar to the one used for a unit annuity plan.

The same sort of right for the insurance company to change the schedule of rates at which each premium is applied to buy a deferred annuity benefit is included in such a contract as was described for the unit annuity plan.

Deposit Administration Plan

When this plan is used, the employer adopts a definite objective of the pension benefits which he wishes his employees to receive, but, instead of definitely purchasing a pension increment each year for each eligible employee, he makes deposits of an amount which it is estimated (but not guaranteed) by the insurance company will be sufficient for the purpose, and which will be improved at a guaranteed rate of interest pending their application to the purchase of definite benefits. Such application will be made on behalf of an individual employee when he has served a stated number of years or reached a stated age, or both. Only after such application is the employee entitled to a definite guarantee from the insurance company of his accrued benefit. If, as the plan proceeds, it appears that the amount of yearly deposit should be increased, the employer is notified by the insurance company.

The rate of interest at which deposits will be improved, and the scale of rates upon which the application of deposits to purchase accrued benefits will be based, may be guaranteed at issue for the amount of money deposited within the first five contract years. For deposits made thereafter the insurance company can alter the rates.

This type of plan may be desired when the employer expects a heavy turnover among his employees, particularly during their earlier service periods, and wishes to simplify his record keeping and some administrative problems under the contract. It may be combined with employee contributions applied on the money purchase plan.

COMPANY PROBLEMS IN CONDUCTING THE ANNUITY BUSINESS

Any annuity premium, like any insurance premium, is based upon an assumed rate of mortality and rate of interest, from which is calculated a net premium, to which in turn is added an amount, determined by judgment, to provide for expenses and contingencies. It is, of course, the intent of the insurance company to make each class of its contracts self-supporting and it therefore plans its assumptions in such a manner that they take into account some degree of uncertainty concerning future developments.

Let us consider for a moment the rate of interest that has to be assumed for the calculations. Perhaps it is well realized that the relative importance of this part of the assumptions depends upon the type of contract involved. In life insurance, for example, variations in the rate of interest assumed will make little difference to a five year term premium but a great deal of difference in the premium for a ten-payment life policy. In virtually all forms of annuity contracts the rate of interest assumed is of vital importance.

When, therefore, the recent unprecedented drop in the rate of interest earnings on investments occurred, the companies were quick to realize that their annuity rates needed prompt adjustment upward to correspond with a downward change in their interest rate assumptions. A general idea of what these changes have meant to the price of the immediate annuities can be realized from the fact that the upward adjustment in the single premium for a life annuity at age 65 between 1930, when the companies were earning about 5 per cent on their assets, and 1948, when they were earning about 3 per cent, can be roughly approximated as 20 per cent because of the changes in interest assumption alone. This represents the change in the net premium by shifting the interest assumption from 4 per cent to 2 per cent. The corresponding proportionate increase in refund annuity premiums was much greater, due to the greater influence of the interest factor on such contracts. As stated, this was the effect of interest changes only. The total percentage increase in annuity premiums over the past eighteen years has been substantially greater, due to the necessity for making more conservative mortality assumptions as well.

Since the companies found it desirable to increase their new business rates in this way, it will be appreciated that they also felt it desirable to increase the reserves held on their old annuity business in order that these reserves might correspond with a more conservative interest rate than had been assumed in their original premiums. Over the past ten years this strengthening of annuity reserves has been substantial. The setting aside of these additional reserves put no great strain on the surplus positions of the companies, because as investment interest rates decreased many corporations whose bonds were held by the companies paid substantial premiums in order to retire them and to refinance them at the lower interest rates then current. The aggregates of the investment profits thus realized by the life insurance companies were very substantial and were the result of the same conditions, of course, that made necessary the strengthening of reserves.

It is more necessary with annuities than with life insurance to adopt an interest rate assumption which will be realized during the existence of the contracts. History indicates that under a life insurance contract, when you have once determined the mortality assumption on a basis which gives the company a reasonable safety margin over its recent experience, the mortality margin will increase with the passage of time. This is due to the fact that, except for temporary interruptions such as come from epidemics and war, death rates have persistently declined from one period to the next. No doubt the reasons for this decline are the advances steadily made in medical knowledge and skill and in public health measures. But, however we may apportion the credit, this process has been going on from the time when data from the census and death registrations have permitted knowledge of the facts.

The increasing mortality margins in life insurance policies have furnished a cushion which is of great importance in the event that the rate of interest earnings falls below the rate assumed in the premium calculations, and this cushion may continue to make such life insurance policies fully self-supporting despite a moderate degree of interest deficiency. In the case of annuities the situation is quite the reverse. If a company bases its mortality assumption on its recent experience, it can be virtually certain that during the period when the contracts will be in effect the mortality rates experienced will fall further and further below the rates assumed. In other words, it will pay more in benefits than it counted upon. Hence, instead of having a mortality cushion to rest upon to meet possible interest deficiencies, the company will need an interest cushion with which to meet inadequate longevity assumptions. One may ask at this point whether a mortality safety margin cannot be used in annuities, to which the answer may be made that this is the intention of modern actuaries. But even when such a margin is used, we know that the margin will narrow throughout the duration of the contracts and may disappear before they are terminated. It is for such reasons that, viewing the combined effect of mortality and interest assumptions and the total safety margins resulting therefrom, it has become common practice to use a lower rate of interest in calculating annuity premiums than the rate used for life insurance premiums. At the present time the interest rate used for annuities is commonly 2 per cent or $2\frac{1}{4}$ per cent.

Despite this practical solution of the problem of maintaining safety and equity among classes of policyholders, actuaries are becoming increasingly interested in devising methods by which annuitants' mortality can be forecast into the future so that more accurate methods may be employed if possible. The problem is quite complex. The mortality to be forecast for immediate annuities should apply to the period of twenty-five years or so following issue of the contract. For a deferred annuity of the common type issued, say, at age 35 with annuity payments beginning at 65, the important mortality period will commence thirty years after issue and the mortality to be experienced should be at a lower level than for the immediate annuities issued concurrently. The possible variations between different forms of contract and different ages are numerous. In such a situation any precise method may prove impracticable but the existence of the dilemma is a strong reason for conservative assumptions in dealing with the interest rate until a better method is developed.

Having thus dealt with the general character of management problems, let us look somewhat more closely at a few significant facts about annuitants' mortality under individual contracts.[4] Such annuitants, of course, determine whether to buy or not to buy and we should expect them on the whole to make intelligent use of that choice, in terms of their opinions concerning their own prospects of longevity. And so they do. Experience under immediate annuities indicates that their mortality is noticeably low for their ages as compared with the general population. For two or three years after issue, their mortality is particularly favorable. Females experience much lower mortality than males, so much so that to protect itself a company must distinguish between the sexes in its premium rates. If a company were not to make that distinction, its rates would become bargains for females and too high for males, with the result that it might well become overloaded with female buyers and experience a scarcity of male buyers. In that event its mortality assumption, based on any averaging of buyers, would become deficient. In current practice an approximate distinction is made by charging for a female a rate which is the same as that for a male who is five years younger.

Purchasers also follow their own self-interest intelligently in selecting the type of immediate annuity which they buy. Thus there is experienced lower mortality among annuitants having

[4] A more extended reference to this subject is made in the author's article "Mortality Among Annuitants" in *The Journal of the American Society of Chartered Life Underwriters*, Sept., 1948.

regular life annuities than among those having refund annuities. So it will be seen that there is no such thing as an inherent rate of mortality applicable to all annuitants but that the mortality experienced will be determined to no small degree by the incentives of self-selection.

Occasionally the question is asked why a company does not give a better annuity return on a physically impaired life than on one not impaired. The presumption is that such lives would be subjected to medical examination to determine their conditions. The experiment has been tried but the practice is virtually nonexistent at present. The fact is that a company would have great difficulty in protecting itself from being imposed upon, particularly with respect to subjective symptoms of impairment which could not be objectively tested; and even when the experiment has been tried, it is reported to have been a disappointment in view of the few impairments which could be clearly measured for this purpose. It is now practically universal practice to quote one set of rates and simply to leave it to individuals to buy that contract or not, as they may wish.

The home office of a life insurance company, in handling the applications for annuities, runs into a number of practical problems. Not the least of these is to be able to confirm authoritatively the stated age of an applicant for an individual annuity. But such problems are matters of detail rather than of principle and we shall not prolong this paper to discuss them.

Let me conclude by observing that our day is one of great emphasis upon providing for the retirement period of life. The mechanisms used for that purpose are already of many kinds, of which those provided by life insurance companies are a prominent part. In rendering the service of providing for retirement benefits, the life insurance companies have demonstrated their capacity to function effectively in a free economy with security in the results and without subsidy. In a country where that part of the population which is unproductive because of old age is on the rise and will continue to increase for a long period at least, this function of the life insurance companies may become of ever increasing importance in serving the public interest.

CHAPTER VII

DEVELOPMENT OF DISABILITY BENEFITS IN LIFE INSURANCE CONTRACTS

By Joseph B. Maclean, F.S.A., F.I.A., F.F.A.*

Company practice in regard to the inclusion of disability benefits in life insurance policies was radically changed in 1932. Only minor developments have occurred since that time.

DEVELOPMENTS UP TO 1932

Disability benefits, whether waiver of premium only or waiver of premium and income benefits, were originally payable only in event of disability that was both *total* and *permanent*. Premiums were at first based on the Hunter Disability Table which was prepared for that purpose but which, of course, did not reflect actual experience in the companies since such experience was then nonexistent. The need for a disability table which would reflect company experience was realized at an early stage. This was partly because it soon became evident that the rates of total and permanent disability experienced by the companies were generally higher than those in the Hunter Table but chiefly because of the adoption of the "presumptive clause."

The presumptive clause under which *total* disability was presumed to be *permanent* (for the purpose of paying benefits) after it had continued for a specified period (at first ninety days) completely altered the character of the coverage and rendered the Hunter Table entirely inapplicable. No table existed, however, which showed the rates of disability when defined as "total disability lasting for at least three months." The companies which adopted this new and expanded type of coverage had to make the best estimates they could as to the premium rates

* Former Vice President and Actuary, The Mutual Life Insurance Co. of N. Y., Past President, The Actuarial Society of America.

100

required for that particular kind of disability. In doing so they made use of available statistics under accident and health policies and long-term sickness benefits paid by some of the fraternal orders. One such source was the "Manchester Unity" Sickness Tables which showed the experience of a large British fraternal order and which had been analyzed by duration of "sickness."

None of these sources of information as to the rates of long-term *total* disability was satisfactory as a measure of life insurance company experience and it was soon realized that the only safe basis would be a table constructed from the actual experience of the companies issuing the new type of disability coverage. There were, however, two serious obstacles to the preparation of such a table. The first of these was the fact that policies with a "presumptive clause" had been issued for only a few years. The rates of disability under these policies, therefore, reflected only the experience of the first few policy years following selection and gave very little indication of what the *ultimate* disability rates would be, while there was no adequate experience as to the *duration of claims,* i.e., the rates of death and recovery among disabled lives, since all existing claims under these policies were of very short duration. It was obvious that these latter rates would be quite different from the rates of death and recovery among those who were actually both totally and permanently disabled.

The second difficulty in constructing suitable tables was the lack of uniformity which had existed both as to the *terms* of the disability provision, and as to the *administration* of the benefits. For example, under the contracts of some companies there was no limitation on the dating back of benefit payments where notice of disability had been delayed, while in other companies there was such a limitation. Again, some companies had been much more liberal than others in regard to the admission of claims under these "presumptive clause" policies, or had exercised less stringency in supervising and terminating claims where recovery seemed to have taken place. This lack of uniformity resulted, of course, in substantially different experience in some companies as compared with others.

New tables were, however, prepared and published in 1926. The difficulty arising from lack of uniformity in contract pro-

visions or practice was met by preparing separate tables from
the experience of those companies with a relatively strict administrative practice (the "Class II Table") and those with a generally more liberal practice (the "Class III Table"). The Class II
Table never came into general use but the Class III Table became
the standard table for presumptive clause policies after 1926 and
still remains (in 1949) the standard basis for reserves so far as
the requirements of the various states are concerned. The companies actually used the Class III Table for premium rates for
only a few years because, as experience developed, the rates of
disability by that table were found to be too low. In 1932, as we
shall see later, the companies generally adopted a modification
of the Class III Table under which the rates of disability were
arbitrarily increased by percentages graded by age and which
corresponded to the actual experience.

These difficulties, due largely to lack of uniformity, in obtaining a satisfactory basis of operations, resulted in the adoption
in 1930 by most of the states of the so-called "Standard Provisions" for disability benefits. In addition to the impossibility of
deriving uniform experience rates of disability and of death or recovery among disabled lives, where coverage was not uniform,
it was evidently undesirable from a practical standpoint that a
disabled policyholder should be entitled to collect benefits from
one company and not from another. Where this situation occurred because of the greater care or severity of administration
in a particular company (rather than from differences in the
contract provisions), nothing could be done about it since the
company was entitled to administer the benefits in accordance
with its best judgment and in the interests of all its policyholders.
It was, however, possible to make the coverage more uniform so
far as the general terms of the contract were concerned. This
was supposed to be the objective of the standard provisions.

These provisions did eliminate a good many of the elements
of difference in coverage but did not actually require uniformity
in all respects. For example, in one of the most important elements of coverage, namely, the length of the presumptive period,
the standard provisions are not "standard" but permit any presumptive period from four months to a year. Obviously, the experience under a four-month period would be radically different

from that under a twelve-month period. Fortunately there was, in fact, a uniform adoption of a four-month (later changed to six-month) presumptive period by practically all companies.

It was believed, no doubt, or hoped, that the adoption of the Class III Table, together with the standard provisions, would cure all the ills which had troubled the disability business. These combined changes took effect at the beginning of 1930. Unfortunately, just as preparations were being made to put these changes into effect, the country became involved in the great economic depression which was to last for several years, and the results of which forced the companies to revise entirely their ideas as to disability coverage.

As we now know, disability claim experience is very closely correlated with the economic cycle and, in times of severe economic depression, disability insurance becomes, to a large extent, unemployment insurance. The companies had been operating in a long period of economic prosperity and, even so, incurring losses because of lack of knowledge of the risk, of the cost of coverage, and of the administrative methods required. When the depression struck, claims increased enormously. In the early 1930's the losses incurred by many companies were such as to call for an entirely new appraisal of the situation and to convince the companies that the changes just made (adoption of the Class III Table and the standard provisions) were very far from sufficient to put the business on a satisfactory basis. It was realized that much more drastic action was required.

Changes Made in 1932

The most far-reaching changes were made in regard to *income* benefits.

A majority of the principal companies ceased altogether to issue policies with income benefits. Most of those which continued to provide such benefits made the following changes:

(1) reduction of the terminating age for coverage from 60 to 55;

(2) reduction of the monthly income per $1,000 of face amount from $10 to $5;

(3) increase in the presumptive period for "permanent disability" from four months to six months;

(4) a change in the basis for calculation of premiums from the Class III Table to the modification of that table referred to above.

In addition, nearly all of the companies which continued disability income benefits limited their issue to male lives only. In the case of group life insurance, the installment disability benefit —which had become a standard feature of group insurance—was discontinued.

Experience where the benefit was restricted to the waiver of premium had been far less unsatisfactory than under the combined waiver and income benefits. Practically all companies decided to continue the issue of policies with the waiver benefit and to retain for such coverage the same terminating age as formerly, namely 60, but with the increased "waiting period" of six months instead of four months. In addition, the premium rates were increased, as in the case of income benefits, and women were, in nearly all companies, charged a higher rate than men, either 150 or 200 per cent of the male premium rate. Waiver benefits were, in general, limited to single, self-supporting women.

In Canada many companies continued to issue policies with a disability income provision but under which the income benefit was both *decreasing* and *temporary*. In many cases the income benefit per $1,000 of face amount was $10 monthly for fifty months, followed by $5 monthly for one hundred months, with payment of the face amount of the policy at the end of one hundred and fifty months, if the insured were still alive and disabled. This form of benefit, while having considerable advantage from the company's point of view, is obviously not an ideal form of insurance protection from the policyholder's point of view—at least where total disability actually exists and is of long duration. As noted later, this type of temporary decreasing income benefit was pretty generally abandoned at a later date.

DEVELOPMENTS FROM 1932 TO 1948

The period from 1932 to 1948 was marked by (1) a general improvement in disability experience with substantial reduction in annual losses or, in some cases, even the substitution of gains for losses; (2) more or less constant pressure from the field, and from other directions, on the companies to resume or to liberalize the issue of income benefits; (3) practically no change in the attitude of the companies.

Improved experience resulted chiefly from increasingly favorable economic conditions during this period and from more stringent administration both as to the admission and the review (continuation) of claims. The terms of the contract which had formerly been interpreted and applied in a rather liberal manner were more rigidly enforced—even where this involved an increase in the number of lawsuits—and greater care was taken in checking up on the continued existence of disability, so that many claims have been terminated at an earlier date than would formerly have been the case. The companies have acquired more knowledge of and experience with this type of business and are better able to administer it profitably.

The generally lower losses shown by the companies in their "gain and loss exhibits" have also been due to the gradual running off of the older and more unfavorable types of contracts which had been written at inadequate premium rates and also to the substantial strengthening of disability reserves which has taken place in most companies during this period. Contracts issued since 1932 have, in general, not resulted in loss, while the effect of adding a substantial amount to disability reserves on older contracts is to reduce the future annual losses under these contracts because of provision for higher rates of disability and the additional interest earnings on the higher reserves.

Improved experience and the general elimination of large annual losses have led to some pressure for a more liberal practice and attitude in regard to income benefits in new policies. The "standard" monthly income benefit in those companies which continued to issue income benefits, viz: $5 per $1,000 face amount, may very well be regarded as too low. Thus, the policyholder who can afford to buy, say, a $25,000 policy, is not likely to consider himself adequately insured against disability by a monthly benefit of $125. It is natural that life insurance agents, and the public, should feel that, if the companies are going to offer this type of insurance protection, it should be on a more realistic basis in relation to loss of income. There is much to be said for that point of view. On the other hand, it is not difficult to understand that the companies are rather reluctant to embark again on a venture which was so disastrous in the past, even where increased knowledge and experience indicate that former errors could be avoided. At any rate there has, as yet, been very little indication of an intention on the part of the companies to expand or liberalize in regard to income benefits. Reference will be made later to some factors which may affect this situation.

There are a few other developments of this period to which some reference may be made. The first of these is negative in character and is the nonadoption by companies generally of the "indemnity" type of disability income provision which was introduced by one large company. The distinctive features of this type of benefit provision are that the amount of income payable in event of disability (1) is not fixed by the maximum amount stated in the policy but is related to the earned income during a specified period prior to claim, and (2) is subject to "pro rate" on account of any other existing disability coverage. There is no question that this type of provision is the most logical and the only one which will eliminate one of the most important causes of loss under disability insurance as now practiced, namely, over-insurance. However, the apparent impossibility of securing the uniform adoption of such a provision by all companies—which, if not essential, is at least highly desirable in order to make such a plan workable to a satisfactory extent—together with other practical objections, has prevented the general adoption of an *indemnity* basis for disability insurance. There seems to be no inclination to experiment with this type of disability provision.

A recent change which has been made in the new contracts of a number of companies relates to the provision in the disability clause as to the effect of war service. Contracts issued during or prior to World War II generally provided that in event of military or naval service in time of war, the disability provision would be automatically terminated, or, in some cases, suspended. Experience during and since the war showed that such a provision resulted in some rather serious practical difficulties. For example, in the case of provision for termination, the company was frequently not notified of the insured's entry in service and continued to accept premiums for the disability benefits. This might not be discovered until after the termination of military service and sometimes only at a much later date when a claim was submitted for which the company was not legally liable. Another difficulty was in connection with the reinstatement of a terminated provision after termination of service. Many applicants for reinstatement were not then insurable for disability benefits under the company's regular rules, but there might be doubt as to whether the impairment was or was not war-caused. Such doubts, plus patriotic considerations, made it desirable for the companies to reinstate benefits on many poor risks and there was, of course, some "anti-selection" in the applications for reinstatement.

In the case of suspension another difficulty was that, while the company automatically resumed the risk upon termination of service, it was not usually feasible to collect any premium until the next premium due date so that, in the aggregate, a substantial amount of coverage had to be given without consideration.

In view of these and similar practical difficulties, many companies are now simply excluding the risk, i.e., providing that benefits are not payable on account of disabilities resulting from war service—the provision remaining otherwise in full force with premiums continuing to be payable.

A development of some importance during the period under consideration has been the apparent establishment by numerous legal decisions (notably Rhine *v.* New York Life and Rubin *v.* Metropolitan Life) that since the disability provision is a *part* of the life insurance contract, and not a *separate* contract (even when the provision is in the form of a "rider" attached to the policy), dividends on the policy may take into account gains or losses from disability. In other words, a lower (or higher) dividend per $1,000 may be paid on a policy *with* disability benefits than on a policy otherwise identical but *not* containing provision for such benefits. The practice of making such a distinction in dividends was adopted by some of the larger companies in the early 1930's and seems to be entirely sound but was not followed by all companies.

CURRENT PRACTICE

The current practice of thirty large companies in regard to the issue of disability benefits is tabulated in the Appendix. This shows, as already noted, that there have been no radical changes since 1932.

It will be noted that none of the ten largest companies issues policies with income benefits and that only eleven of the thirty do so. Of the eleven, nine give coverage to age 55 and only two (of which one is the company having the indemnity type of clause) give coverage to 60. In seven companies the income benefit is still $5 monthly, payable until death or recovery. One (the "indemnity" company) pays $10. Two pay a *decreasing* income (also *temporary* in one company) and one has a temporary income to 65 with payment of the face amount at that time if the insured is still alive and disabled.

Three of these companies issue income benefits to women but at higher premium rates and either with an earlier termination age, a lower monthly income, or both.

All thirty companies issue policies with a waiver benefit only and with coverage to age 60. The principal differences, so far as waiver of premium is concerned, are in regard to the insurance of women. Three companies now offer women waiver benefits at the same premium rates as men; seven charge 50 per cent more, and eighteen charge 100 per cent more. The remainder have special (higher) premium scales for women. In eight companies the waiver provision is cancelled in event of marriage and practically no company issues the waiver benefit to other than single, self-supporting women.

In Canada, most companies issuing income benefits now have the "U.S. type" of provision, that is, coverage to 55 and monthly income of $5 for *life*. Four Canadian companies pay $10 monthly to age 65, with payment of face amount at 65, coverage continuing only to 55.

In regard to group insurance, there seems to be a tendency towards reestablishing the "instalment disability benefit" which was more or less standard in group policies prior to 1932. However, this benefit is apparently being allowed only in selected cases and subject to payment of an extra premium. Formerly no additional premium was charged for the disability benefit (payment of the face amount in installments).

FUTURE DEVELOPMENTS

While there are some important factors which may lead to a more general issue of income disability benefits as time goes on, and to greater liberality in the terms of the disability provision, it does not seem very likely that there will be any important developments along this line in the immediate future. The heavy losses sustained in the past and the many practical difficulties inherent in the administration of this type of coverage are still very much in the minds of company officers and boards of directors. Although a great deal has been learned by experience, both as to costs and as to the requirements for successful administration, it is to be expected that those companies which concluded that income disability benefits were a losing proposition and abandoned their issue altogether, will go rather slowly in considering any reversal of that action.

Some of the factors which may affect this situation are: (1) improved experience, in recent years, even under the older types of contracts, due chiefly to favorable economic conditions and the greater strictness in administration and interpretation of contract terms; (2) greater knowledge of the *cost*; (3) pressure of competition and the general need and demand for more adequate protection against long continued disablement; and, perhaps most important of all, (4) the desirability of demonstrating that this important insurance need can be met by private enterprise.

As regards improved experience and reduction in disability losses, there is, of course, some natural tendency to discount the experience of the past or, at least, to believe that with greater knowledge past errors and losses can be avoided. There is a great deal of justification for that belief. A fundamental requirement of successful operation, which was largely absent in the earlier stages of development, is the ability to measure the risk and to arrive at adequate premium rates. The comparative uniformity in terms of coverage which has existed for about the past twenty years, and the volume of statistical data now available for the construction of reliable disability tables, furnish a satisfactory basis for determining probable cost and, together with greater knowledge of the administrative measures required, should virtually eliminate the possibility of such losses as were formerly sustained.

Competition and the general inadequacy of the type of income benefits now available result also in more or less continuous pressure for further consideration and expansion and this may eventually have some effect.

The proposals to extend the Old Age and Survivors Insurance provision of the Social Security law to include long-term disability benefits, which are, perhaps, now more likely than before to be adopted in the near future, certainly require that the companies review all the possibilities very carefully. No extension of coverage which would be practical or possible for the companies could, however, cover all the classes of the population which would be included in any federal plan, but it is important that any federal coverage should be limited to minimum benefits and that the companies should be able to supply, at least to the majority of applicants, adequate supplementary coverage above the subsistence level supplied by a federal plan.

Any income disability coverage which is to be reasonably adequate and satisfactory would seem to require a monthly benefit of $10, rather than $5 per $1,000 of face amount, and to give protection up to age 65 rather than 55. Possibly future developments may be along that line with provision for a *temporary* income, ceasing at 65 (and with payment of the face amount of the policy at 65 if still disabled), rather than an income payable until death or recovery. Under such a benefit the income settlements of the face amount available at 65 could replace the disability income. The benefit described would, however, be more costly than the present "standard" disability income benefit, viz., coverage to 55 with a $5 monthly income until death or recovery.

A minor future development may be in greater liberality in regard to the *waiver* benefit for women. Experience under *income* benefits was definitely much worse for women than for men but under suitable limitations (e.g., to single self-supporting women) the experience under the waiver benefit has, in many cases, been quite favorable. Some companies have reduced the extra charge for women and a few now charge the same rates as for men.

PROPOSED EXTENSION OF O.A.S.I.

Although we are considering only disability benefits in life insurance policies, the effect on these of any extension of the Old Age and Survivors Insurance under the federal Social Security law may be considerable, so that it is not inappropriate to refer briefly to the proposals for extending O.A.S.I. by the inclusion of long term disability benefits.

It seems very probable that there will soon be such an extension. A majority of the Advisory Council on Social Security appointed by the Finance Committee of the Senate was favorable to an extension on some basis. Many of those who are best informed on social legislation feel, however, that there are grave dangers in any such plan on the federal level.

This feeling arises in part from the special characteristics of the disability risk which call for unusual care in administration. It is to be remembered that under any federal plan there would be no *selection*. All persons within the scope of the law would be covered, including many who would be uninsurable for disability benefits on any terms in the companies. The amount of fraud and malingering, inseparable from this type of insurance, would undoubtedly be very great under a federal plan, particularly if the levels of benefits collectible were not far below the amounts which could be earned by working—after deducting the various savings made by the non-worker, including income taxes, payroll deductions and daily overhead. Unless the margin of net work income over benefits should be large, many persons would, no doubt, prefer to accept the lower disability income with its greater security and freedom from the need to work rather than the larger income obtainable by working.

In addition to these and other similar administrative problems, there are dangers arising from political considerations. There would certainly be political pressure on the administrative officials to allow or continue benefits in many cases where bene-

APPENDIX

Summary of Current Practice of 30 Large Companies
as to the issue of

DISABILITY INCOME AND WAIVER OF PREMIUM BENEFITS
(November 1948)

Company	Waiver of Premium	Income	Monthly Amount	Terminating Age of Coverage	Income to Women	Waiver of Premium Rates for Women
Metropolitan	Yes	No				100%
Prudential	"	"				100
Equitable Life, New York	"	"				200 (5)
New York Life	"	"				200 (9)
John Hancock Mutual	"	"				200 (6)
Travelers	"	"				200 (6)
Aetna	"	"				Higher
Northwestern Mutual	"	"				150 (5)
Mutual Life, N. Y.	"	"				100
Sun Life, Canada	"	"				200 (6)
Lincoln National	"	Yes	$ 5.00	55		150
Massachusetts Mutual	"	"	5.00	55		150
Mutual Benefit	"	"	10.00	60 (Women Age 55)	$ 5.00	150 (8)
Penn Mutual	"	"	5.00	55		200 (8)
New England Mutual	"	No				200 (6)
Connecticut General	"	"				Higher (10)
Western and Southern	"	"				200 (7)
National Life and Accident	"	Yes	(1)	55		200 (6)
Connecticut Mutual	"	No				Higher (8)
American National	"					200 (8)

(Table continued on following page)

Company							
Occidental, Cal.	Yes	Yes	(3)	60 (Women Age 55)	(3)	150	(6)
London Life	"	"	(2)	55 (Women Age 50)	(5) $ 5.00(6)	200	(5)
						200	(6)
Union Central	"	No		55		200	(8)
Bankers, Iowa	"	Yes	5.00	55		200	(5)
Provident Mutual	"	"	5.00			150	(8)
Canada Life	"	No		55		200	(6)
Life Ins. Co. of Virginia	"	"	5.00	55		200	(8)
Manufacturers	"	"	5.00 (4)			200	(6)
Great West	"	Yes				200	(6)
Phoenix Mutual	"	"				150	(8)
Totals	30	11	$ 5-7 Cos. 10-1 " Spec.-3 "	Men Women 55-9 Cos. 55-2 Cos. 60-2 " 50-1 "	$ 5-2 Cos. Spec.-1 "	100%-3 Cos. 150 -7 " 200 -18 " Spec. -3 "	

NOTES

(1) $10 for 30 months, $5 for an additional 60 months.
(2) Issues policies with both $5 and $10 income. Face Amount at 65 if not already matured.
(3) $10 monthly income to 60, $5 thereafter except Endowment Life Income $10 to maturity.
(4) $2.50 after maturity of endowments.
(5) Self-supporting only.
(6) Single self-supporting only.
(7) Single women only.
(8) Single self-supporting, canceled on marriage.
(9) Receiving earned income.
(10) Single, canceled at marriage, except in New York.

fits might not actually be payable under the qualifying conditions of the law. Emphasis would be placed on the legal right to benefits rather than on the qualifying conditions. In periods of favorable experience or of inflation there would be agitation to increase the scale of benefit payments beyond what was safe or appropriate, while under unfavorable economic conditions the plan would almost certainly function to a large extent as unemployment rather than disability insurance.

Where experience proves the unsoundness of a disability insurance plan operated commercially, the company can modify the plan or discontinue it—as many companies did in 1932. A government plan is likely to be modified only in one way, by increasing the benefits and by greater liberality, while to discontinue such a plan is virtually impossible. The solvency or insolvency of the plan would make little difference in view of the prevailing idea that federal funds are unlimited.

All this is not to say that a federal plan of disability insurance is impossible. But it does mean that if the plan is to work out as originally contemplated, it must be administered intelligently, honestly and rigorously, and it must be kept "out of politics." Otherwise, it could very easily and quickly get out of hand with serious financial consequences, to say nothing of other, perhaps equal or more serious, social consequences on the morale of the nation.

CHAPTER VIII

MODERN INDUSTRIAL LIFE INSURANCE

By Malvin E. Davis, F.S.A., A.C.A.S.*

Literature on the subject of life insurance is quite voluminous, but the great bulk of it deals solely or principally with the ordinary branch of the business in which life insurance is sold in amounts of $1,000 or more with premiums on an annual, semi-annual, quarterly and, in some cases, monthly basis. This insurance, however, does not fit the circumstances and needs of many families of modest income.

For such families was the industrial branch of the business developed and it continues to be the practical means of obtaining the benefits of legal reserve life insurance. In this branch, insurance is provided in units of hundreds rather than thousands of dollars. Each individual premium payment is made as small as possible by having the premium generally payable in weekly instalments, although some companies sell the larger industrial policies on a monthly-premium basis. Furthermore, the payment of the premium is made as convenient as possible by providing the additional service of having agents periodically call at the policyholders' homes to collect the premiums. Although the industrial branch of the life insurance business has received little specific attention in insurance literature, it is a very important part of the life insurance protection of the American public.

At the end of 1948, legal reserve companies in the United States were providing life insurance protection totaling $207 billion. Of this amount, more than $32½ billion was industrial life insurance. Considering the number of persons protected, the importance of the industrial branch is even more pronounced. Of the estimated 78 million American life insurance policyholders, about two-thirds own industrial policies—one out of every three persons in the nation.

* Actuary, Metropolitan Life Insurance Company.

Industrial life insurance has brought to a large part of our population the benefits of individual life insurance. This branch, which makes life insurance conveniently available to families of moderate income, provides large aggregate sums to its policyholders each year at times when the money is most needed.

During the past five years, more than one billion dollars has been paid to families in the United States in death benefits on industrial policies. The value of these sums, coming as they do in time of great need, can hardly be overestimated. But these payments at death represent only part of the service rendered by industrial life insurance.

During these same five years, about three-fourths of a billion dollars was paid in maturing industrial endowments. These endowment policies have been a popular form of insurance on the lives of children especially, in order to help further their education or aid them in establishing homes of their own.

Even in years when the nation is enjoying a full measure of prosperity, many individual families are faced with financial difficulties. In all too many cases the cash values provided by their industrial policies are their only ready source of financial assistance. During the past five years companies paid about one-half billion dollars in cash values to their industrial policyholders. In times of economic depression there are, of course, many more families that need financial assistance, and the cash values provided by industrial policies play an even greater role. In the year 1932, although the volume of industrial insurance in force then was little more than half that of today, the companies paid almost as much in cash surrender values to their industrial policyholders as they did during the past five years.

Industrial policies also provide a lump sum cash payment in case of disability arising from blindness or loss of limbs. Each month the companies make such payments on more than a thousand policies under which the insured becomes thus disabled.

Industrial policyholders and their beneficiaries are receiving as death benefits, endowment amounts, disability benefits, and cash surrender values over half a billion dollars a year—a significant indication of the important role of industrial life insurance in filling important needs of wage-earning families of the nation.

More than one hundred companies in the United States today

are transacting industrial life insurance. Although the basic principles upon which it is conducted are common to all companies, practices and experiences naturally differ somewhat among them. About two-thirds of the industrial life insurance in force is in three companies that have transacted this business for a longer period and over a much wider area than have the others. These are the Metropolitan, the Prudential, and the John Hancock. This presentation will deal mainly with the practices and experiences of these three companies and will use those of the Metropolitan for illustrative purposes.

Prior to the middle 1920's, industrial insurance was written only on a weekly-premium basis, and ordinary insurance was written only with premiums payable quarterly or less frequently. Although the payment of premiums on a weekly basis is essential to bring insurance within reach of millions of families, it does involve more expense than if the premiums were payable less frequently. Even twenty years ago, the income of many wage earners had increased to the extent that, while still unable to purchase ordinary insurance on the basis then available, they no longer needed to pay their premiums weekly. Some life insurance companies therefore began the practice of accepting ordinary premiums in monthly instalments.

When such insurance is serviced on the premium notice and receipt basis, typical of that used for regular ordinary insurance, the accepting of premiums in monthly instalments becomes unduly expensive when such premiums are quite small in amount. Consequently, companies that do not write industrial insurance, which are commonly referred to as ordinary companies, found it necessary to impose a minimum limit, such as ten dollars, on the size of monthly premiums that they would accept.

Companies that transact industrial as well as ordinary insurance, which are commonly referred to as "combination" companies, similarly found it necessary to impose that limit in the case of those policies which are serviced on the premium notice and receipt basis. However, the combination companies could also issue policies with monthly premiums of less than ten dollars by servicing them in a manner similar to that used for their weekly-premium industrial policies. They were thereby able to extend the issue of monthly-premium insurance to amounts less than $1,000. The large combination companies are thus able to offer insurance in amounts and with premium payment frequencies suited to the needs of every income level of the population.

Some combination companies issue their monthly-premium policies for less than $1,000 as a form of ordinary policy, while others issue them as industrial contracts. That is more a matter of administrative facility for the company than of significance to the policyholders. The cost of this insurance is about the same in either case and the provisions of modern ordinary and industrial policies are very much alike.

POLICY PROVISIONS

An indication of the limited extent to which modern ordinary and industrial policy provisions differ can be obtained from a comparison of such policies currently issued by the Metropolitan. Certain provisions which are quite valuable in policies for larger amounts are unsuited to policies for small amounts of insurance, and are omitted from industrial policies. For instance, such policies do not generally contain a provision for policy loans, since such loans would naturally be quite small and the expense of servicing very small loans would be disproportionate to the value of loans to the policyholders. In the case of the Metropolitan, its $750 monthly-premium industrial policies contain loan privileges and all of its other industrial policies (which are for smaller amounts) do not.

Similarly, a provision for a choice as to the form in which dividends on participating policies might be taken would increase unduly the expenses on industrial policies, without compensating benefit to policyholders. Some policies provide that their dividends will be paid in the form of a credit toward premiums and others that the dividends will be paid in the form of paid-up additions to the sum insured.

Settlement options, which are very useful to the holders of the larger amounts of insurance, would be of little worth in connection with policies for small amounts and are generally omitted from industrial policies. In the case of the Metropolitan, only

its $750 monthly-premium industrial policies contain options of
this nature, and they are more limited than in ordinary policies.
On the other hand, the fact that industrial policies are for
smaller amounts than ordinary policies makes it possible to grant
certain additional benefits, and in some cases more liberal treatment, to industrial policyholders.

Industrial policies of this company do not include the application as part of the contract; they may be contested only within
one year of issue, and then only if the insured has undergone
medical treatment for a serious physical condition within two
years prior to issue and has not disclosed that fact in his application. It is not necessary for the applicant to determine whether
an ailment for which he had medical attention was serious or
not. He merely reports the fact that he had medical attention,
giving the date, nature of the ailment or treatment, its duration,
and the name of the attending physician or the hospital. Thereafter, it is the responsibility of the company to determine
whether further examination is required. This provision for
possible contesting of an industrial claim is considerably more
liberal to the policyholder than is possible for policies of larger
amounts, which contain the application as part of the contract
and may be contested within two years of issue for any material
misstatement in the application. Industrial policies do not contain a suicide restriction since it is not necessary in policies for
these smaller amounts.

Industrial policies provide, without specific extra premium
charge, an additional accidental means death benefit which is
the same as the double indemnity benefit that can be purchased
with ordinary insurance. The ordinary policies of this company
include a benefit under which the premium payments are waived
when the insured is totally and permanently disabled. Such a
benefit is also included, without specific extra premium therefor,
in its $750 monthly-premium industrial policies. It is not in-
cluded in its other industrial policies because no means has as
yet been developed whereby such a benefit could be administered
efficiently and economically when the individual premiums to be
waived are very small. The industrial policies, however, do provide, without specific extra premium charge, a benefit in the
event of loss of eyesight or limbs. If, as a result of accident or

disease, the insured suffers the loss by severance of both hands or both feet, or one hand and one foot, or the loss of the sight of both eyes, the company will pay a sum equal to the amount of insurance and continue the original policy in force for its full amount without further payment of premiums. If the insured loses one hand or one foot, then one-half the amount of insurance will be paid in cash and the original insurance continued without payment of future premiums.

The industrial policies provide for the naming of a beneficiary, and also contain a facility-of-payment clause which permits payment to persons of specified classes if the designated beneficiary is the estate, or a minor or incompetent, or predeceased the insured, or fails to make claim within a period of 60 days. This clause permits the company to make speedy payment to the proper parties, without forcing the payee to incur the expense, trouble and delay of having an administrator or guardian appointed. A clause is also contained in industrial policies whereby the insured can return his policy within a few weeks after issue, if he is not fully satisfied with the contract, and receive a refund of the premiums paid.

An important service for industrial families is the personal call of the agent to receive premiums, but this service involves expense. Although most industrial policyholders need and want the agent's service in receiving premiums, there are many who can and are willing to do without it. The latter may reduce the cost of their weekly-premium insurance by paying premiums directly. The policy provides that, if premiums are paid continuously, without default beyond the grace period, for a period of one year to an office of the company that maintains an account for receiving direct payments, the company will refund at the end of the year 10 per cent of the total year's premiums.

For otherwise identical policies, those with weekly premiums must cost somewhat more than those with monthly premiums, principally because of the greater expense of handling the smaller and more frequent premium payments. Some policyholders for whom the weekly basis is at first the most suitable may later find that they can pay in less frequent instalments. The company's weekly-premium policies assure the policyholder the privilege of converting such policies to any policy with less frequent premium payments that is regularly issued by the company. In fairness to those already insured in the class in which the new policy is to be included, such policyholders must submit satisfactory evidence of insurability in accordance with the standards for that class and the amount of insurance involved must be at least the minimum issued in that class.

Industrial policies, like ordinary, provide for nonforfeiture values in case the policyholder defaults in payment of premiums. The nonforfeiture values are determined in exactly the same way for both classes of policies, except that the ordinary values reflect mortality experience under ordinary insurance, while the industrial values reflect mortality under industrial policies.

A nonforfeiture value in the form of extended term insurance is provided automatically, on both industrial and ordinary policies, after premiums have been paid for a half-year. After premiums have been paid for a certain minimum period, the industrial as well as the ordinary policies provide that the nonforfeiture value may be taken in the form of cash or as paid-up life or endowment insurance for a reduced amount, instead of as extended term insurance. In the case of the ordinary policies the minimum period after which such a choice is offered is two years; in the case of industrial it is three years, because prior to that time the amount of cash value on a small policy is necessarily quite small and the expense of making such payments would be disproportionate.

This completes the list of noteworthy differences between the modern industrial and ordinary policy contract. In all other respects the provisions of the two contracts are practically identical. The differences that do exist, as just described, are the result of developing each contract to best serve its policyholders.

SELECTION OF RISKS

Members of the lower income groups experience an inherently higher death rate than those of the same sex and age that are insured under ordinary policies. In order that industrial insurance may be available to practically everyone who is not in seriously impaired health, a broader—more liberal—basis of acceptance is employed for industrial than for standard ordinary insurance. Furthermore, for the smaller amounts characteristic of industrial policies a simple and inexpensive underwriting procedure is essential. Medical examination is required in fewer cases, and when required is briefer and less expensive than that needed for ordinary insurance. Many applicants who are acceptable for industrial insurance at its standard premium rates would be regarded as substandard for ordinary insurance because of their occupation, physical condition, or personal health history.

FIELD FORCE ORGANIZATION

The field force of a company that does not transact industrial insurance may operate under either a "branch office" or "general agency" system, but a company that transacts industrial uses the branch office system. This permits a more direct contact between the management at the home office and the individual agent, and a direct control of the many detailed field services that are required in connection with this branch of the business.

A company transacting industrial life insurance divides the territory in which it operates into a number of areas that are called districts. A district may be part of a large city, a medium-sized city, or a number of neighboring towns. Each district has a manager (or superintendent) in charge, with one or more assistants, and has a public office with a small clerical force.

Each district is subdivided into smaller areas, to each of which an agent is assigned. It is a great help in the efficient servicing of policies, for which the individual premium payments are quite small and made at frequent intervals, that each agent have a prescribed area which is mutually exclusive from areas of other agents of the company. The area assigned to each agent is known as his "debit." The origin of this name stems from the premium accounting system that is used.

PREMIUM ACCOUNTING SYSTEM

This accounting system is entirely different from that typical of ordinary insurance. Advantage is taken of the fact that the weekly premiums all fall due at the same time and that for the convenience of the policyholders an agent calls at their homes to receive them. Each family is provided with a premium receipt book in which the agent receipts for the premiums. The agent carries with him a debit book in which there is a page for each family and which is arranged in the most efficient manner for him to make his rounds. This book contains information about the insurance holdings of the family and in this he also enters a notation about the receipt of the premiums.

The agent does not report the receipt of each premium separately to the home office. Each week he makes up an accounting form in which he begins by charging (i.e., debiting) himself with one week's premium on all the weekly-premium policies in force in his debit. He then reconciles this with the amount of his cash collections by making the necessary adjustments, such as adding the premiums that he has received that were not due in that week, and deducting those that were due but were not paid. Each week the agent is officially notified by the home office of the policies that have been added to his debit or ceased to be in force in it and the up-to-date amount of his debit, which then becomes the initial entry in his account for the following week.

This system permits the company to operate without maintaining a running record at the home office of the premium payments on each individual policy. The home office records do not tell whether the premiums for the current week have been paid or not, but only disclose whether the policy is in force or has been reported for lapse, and if reported for lapse, the date to which premiums were paid. Periodically the agent submits a listing of the policies on which premiums have been paid in advance and those which are in arrears, for audit and other purposes. Audits of each agent's account are made periodically, and various controls are used to assure accuracy in the agent's reporting.

For monthly-premium policies serviced on the debit plan, a similar premium accounting system is used. This debit system of premium accounting is very important to the efficient handling of small premium payments.

Selection and Training of Agents

Providing good insurance service depends to a very large degree on the calibre of the field force. Not every man is suited for such work. Careful attention must be given to selecting the men that are to become agents. They must then be trained for the work and adequately guided by supervision and management. They must be remunerated in a manner that does not permit their financial reward to be in conflict with their giving the best advice and service to their policyholders, and their compensation must be adequate for their services and provide them with an incentive to perform their work well.

Increasing attention has been paid in recent years to the careful selection of agents and to their formalized training before they go out on the debit. Aptitude tests to aid in selecting qualified applicants have been widely used, and prospective agents are carefully screened before their appointment. The Metropolitan has training schools at several centers where the newly appointed agent studies for two weeks. After completing his preliminary schooling, the agent reports to his district office; in some states he is also required to take a state examination for an agent's license. In the district office, training continues under the supervision of the assistant manager, who accompanies him on the debit each day for the first few weeks, and gives him such additional individual instruction as he may require. Then for the succeeding six months he is closely supervised and given special additional instruction as may be needed. Special instruction and correspondence courses are also used in completing the agent's training and education. Many agents, as well as managers and assistant managers, have successfully taken the courses and passed the examinations leading to the designation of Chartered Life Underwriter (C.L.U.).

AGENTS' COMPENSATION

Each of the three largest combination companies has greatly improved its method of compensating field men for selling and servicing industrial and ordinary debit policies over the past two decades. Such compensation includes selling, collection, and conservation commissions.

The basis of the selling commission encourages the agent to sell only insurance that a family can afford to, and probably will, maintain in force. This commission depends on the continued payment of premiums throughout the policy's first year—the period when the normal tendency to lapse is greatest. The rate of sales commission is one-fourth lower for endowments of 30 years or less than for other plans. The sales commission is at the same rate for weekly- as for monthly-premium debit policies, which on the average is about the same as that for regular ordinary policies.

The collection commission is a fixed percentage of the premiums received by the agent. This rate is generally 12 per cent on weekly premiums, and 6 per cent on monthly-debit premiums.

The conservation commission gives the agent a financial incentive to conserve existing insurance. The amount of this commission varies from $3 to $7 a week, depending on the relative lapse rate of the agent's debit business as compared with that for the entire company on debit policies.

During 1948, Metropolitan agents earned an average of about $88 a week, of which three-fourths was for selling and servicing debit insurance. The remainder consisted of earnings on regular ordinary insurance, group insurance, annuities, and personal accident and health insurance.

FAMILY PROGRAMMING

One of the most far-reaching developments in industrial life insurance during recent years has been the increasing attention given to arranging family programs on a sound basis. A basic step in this direction was the introduction of the methods of training and compensating agents in current use. But much more than this has already been done, and constant efforts are being made to devise even better ways of improving the effectiveness of wage-earners' life insurance. Rules have been established to guide agents in selling, and home office underwriters in approving, applications for new insurance, so that proper consideration is given as to whether the insurance would be suitable to the family's needs and circumstances. The following practices of the Metropolitan will illustrate the nature of such programming.

Relation of Premiums to Family Income. A primary consideration in establishing a sound family program of insurance is that the premiums do not require an undue portion of the family's income. In addition to educating its agents to the disadvantages of overinsurance and arranging the basis of compensating agents for new business with the same objective, the company takes other specific steps to avoid the possible oversale of insurance. Information given in the application about the family's income and its premium outlay is considered at the home office, and if the premiums exceed a certain percentage of income, approval of the application is withheld. The limits applied are more rigid for low than for higher incomes.

Distribution of Insurance within the Family. In determining how the money available for premiums should be distributed in purchasing insurance for the various members of the family, a basic principle that is stressed in the training of agents is that the insurance program should be centered around the principal wage earner, since his death will impose the greatest financial burden on the family. Other employed members of the family should next receive consideration in accordance with the financial loss that would be occasioned by their death.

It is not sufficient, however, to insure only the wage earners. In lower-income families the death of the mother of young children necessitates temporary expenditures for their care. Hence, a housewife may well be insured for an amount greater than is necessary for expenses of her last illness and burial. The final illness and funeral costs for a dependent child also present a serious financial problem to these families, which rarely have any appreciable amount of savings.

Since some protection on dependent members of the family is highly desirable, limitations are imposed only to avoid disproportionate amounts. Insurance in excess of $750 on the life of a housewife is generally permitted only if the husband is insured for at least twice (in some instances, three times) as much, or if the housewife's total premium would require only a very small proportion of the husband's income. For other adult dependents, the total amount of insurance is more severely restricted.

Strict limitations have also been placed on the insurance of young children. No weekly premium insurance will be issued on the life of a child under age 10 which would bring the total premium in all companies to more than 25 cents a week. Generally, not even this amount will be issued if the father is not insured. Monthly-premium policies may be written on young children only if the person responsible for the child's support is insured for specified minimum amounts.

Frequency of Premium Payment. The agents who sell weekly-premium life insurance also sell monthly-premium policies and ordinary insurance with premiums payable less frequently. Hence, the agent is able to recommend the particular policy which, in amount of insurance and frequency of premium payment, will be best suited to the amount and frequency of the family's income.

To avoid issuing weekly-premium insurance when a less expensive form is within the family's means, the company will not issue more than $750 of weekly-premium insurance (or $500 if on the 20-payment life plan) on an adult within a period of six months. Limitations are also placed on the total amount of weekly-premium insurance that will be issued on one person. If an applicant already has ordinary insurance, or if he would have more than $1,000 of weekly-premium insurance, the company will not issue a new weekly-premium policy unless supplementary information shows it to be more appropriate than one with less frequent premium payments or the applicant specifically insists on it. Similar rules are followed if the advance deposit at the time of application is substantial enough to suggest that premiums could be paid less often than weekly, or if the weekly premium required for the insurance being applied for exceeds 50 cents. No policy will be issued for more than $1.00 of weekly premium. All applications received at the home office are reviewed by trained clerks who verify that these rules have been complied with.

Plans of Insurance. The two most popular plans of weekly-premium industrial insurance are whole life policies with premiums payable to an advanced age, such as 65 or 75, and 20-year payment life policies.

In the past, 15- and 20-year endowment policies were very popular plans of weekly-premium insurance, particularly for young children. However, the low rates of interest which are currently being earned on life insurance company investments have made these policies less desirable when premiums must be collected weekly. The interest earnings are not then sufficient to meet all expenses and give a reasonable return over the amount paid in premiums. Accordingly, the largest companies have discontinued issuing such endowment policies on a weekly-premium basis, and endowments on a monthly-premium basis are issued only for terms of 20 years or more. When serviced monthly, these policies can still be offered at attractive rates despite current low interest yields, because of the lower expenses involved.

Persistency

The lapse rate of weekly-premium policies has been characteristically higher than that of ordinary policies. To some extent this is a natural consequence of the different frequencies of premium payment—there are many more occasions for a policy to lapse if premiums are payable weekly than if they fall due quarterly or annually. Probably an even more important factor, however, is the income class of the policyholder. Industrial policies are bought by the lower-income groups, whose margins of income over necessary expenditures are usually quite narrow. As a result, they are more affected by financial ups and downs. Even temporary loss of income or suddenly increased expenses may force them to interrupt their insurance programs.

Company efforts to improve the persistency experience on weekly-premium industrial policies have been particularly effective in reducing the lapse rate shortly after issue, when it is most susceptible to improvement. Emphasis on proper selling methods and on sound programming has aided materially in this. In the Metropolitan, the proportion of policies issued which lapse within the first twenty-six weeks has been reduced from 30 per cent in 1935 to 18 per cent in 1939, and to less than 8 per cent in 1948.

At the later policy durations, the persistency rate of industrial policies follows the trend of economic conditions very closely. When conditions are good, the lapse rate is low; when conditions deteriorate, the lapse rate progressively increases. Continuous attention to proper methods of selling and to the conservation of existing policies has a beneficial effect on the lapse rate at all durations, but the business cycle probably is a major influence in renewal years.

A study of the Metropolitan's weekly-premium industrial lapse and surrender rate, excluding policies in their first calendar year, shows that from 1929 to the depth of the great depression in 1932 the lapse rate doubled, from 6.7 per cent to 13.4 per cent. Thereafter, it decreased almost without interruption, except for the economic recession of 1938, to a low in 1944 of only 1.6 per cent, or about one-eighth of the 1932 rate. Beginning late in 1945, postwar readjustment and inflationary conditions have caused some upswing from the abnormally low rates of 1943-1945, but the 1948 rate was still only 3.1 per cent, which is well below prewar levels.

HEALTH AND WELFARE WORK

Two of the large combination companies are offering extensive health services to their industrial policyholders. Such companies have had exceptional opportunities to render service in this respect. Their agents are in frequent contact with the segments of the population that have most needed health education, yet were hardest to reach through the usual educational channels. The companies have also been able to assemble and publish valuable statistical information relating to diseases and causes of death among their millions of policyholders.

The health and welfare programs have consisted of four principal activities: (1) direct health service to sick policyholders by visiting nurses; (2) health education through popular booklets, advertisements, exhibits, films, and radio broadcasts; (3) coöperation with health departments, schools, industries, and other agencies in campaigns aimed at preventing or controlling disease and accidents; and (4) practical demonstrations of disease control, research in medical problems, and financial support of various health projects.

The Metropolitan, which has had the most extensive health and welfare program, has provided more than 100 million nursing visits to policyholders, and has distributed 1.4 billion health and safety pamphlets, in the forty years its program has been in operation. No direct charge is made for these services. During recent years, some curtailment in the nursing services provided has been made appropriate by the increased health knowledge on the part of the general public, and the extension of the services of other agencies in this field. But even in 1948, more than one and a half million nursing visits were made. The company devotes about one per cent of the income of its industrial branch to this service.

Health education and health services by the various interested agencies have been especially productive in extending life among the lower income groups. The improvement in mortality among industrial policyholders has been considerably greater than among those groups insured under ordinary policies. At the turn of the century the death rate among Metropolitan industrial policyholders was about double that among its standard ordinary policyholders. By 1940, the industrial mortality had become only one-fifth greater than ordinary, and there are indications that this ratio has declined even further in more recent years.

EXPENSE

The expenses that may be incurred in transacting industrial insurance by companies operating in New York State, which includes the three largest companies, are limited by statute. Besides limiting the total expenses, the law prescribes certain limitations as to how they may be incurred. Agents' compensation must be determined in advance, first-year commissions on industrial insurance must not exceed those on ordinary monthly-debit insurance, and no bonus may be paid based on the volume of new business sold.

The expense rate on weekly-premium industrial life insurance is, of course, higher than that on annual-premium ordinary policies because of the smaller units of insurance and the more frequent payment of premiums. However, for weekly-premium industrial policyholders who pay premiums direct to a company office and receive the 10 per cent refund on such payments, the expense charge is little greater than for ordinary policies on which premiums are payable monthly.

For instance, a study of Metropolitan's industrial business, made by the New York State insurance department about ten years ago, indicated that the expense charge for those policyholders whose weekly premiums were collected by agents exceeded that on monthly-debit ordinary policies by 13 per cent of the premiums. For those policyholders who paid their weekly premiums direct to the company, the expense charge was greater than that for monthly-debit ordinary policies by only 3 per cent of the premiums. Although this study was made ten years ago, more recent studies have indicated that there has been no significant change in the relative expense charges since that time.

Since the last war there has been an increase in the expense rate of conducting industrial life insurance, just as there has been in the cost of everything else. This has offset operating economies that were accomplished over a number of years. When we compare the current expense rate with that at the turn of the century, however, we find it very materially lower despite the many additional services to policyholders that have been added.

Two major factors in achieving this have been the introduction of monthly-premium policies and the introduction of the refund for direct payment of weekly premiums. At present, about one-third of all weekly premiums are paid directly to the Metropolitan. Even for weekly-premium business on which premiums are collected by agents, however, there has been a material reduction in the expense rate. On such business, the Metropolitan's expense rate is about 15 per cent lower than it was at the turn of the century.

It is interesting to note that even under current conditions of low interest earnings and inflated costs of doing business, the interest earnings credited to industrial policyholders pay for the greater part of the total expense of selling, servicing and administering the insurance. In 1948, the expense charge to Metropolitan industrial policyholders (exclusive of taxes) exceeded the interest credited to their insurance by an amount equal to 4 per cent of their premiums. When one considers that in most cases the money devoted to these premiums would otherwise not have been invested to earn interest, the net cost of obtaining this insurance is indeed quite low in relation to the extensive service the policyholders receive and the benefits they derive from it.

RECENT TRENDS IN WAGE-EARNERS' INSURANCE

Although monetary incomes of wage earners have increased substantially in recent years, weekly-premium insurance continues to be the most appropriate form for a large segment of the population. While more and more wage earners need and can purchase more substantial amounts of insurance on their own lives, the insurance needs of other members of their families are being appropriately met through policies of smaller amounts. The need for at least modest amounts of insurance on the lives of dependents is greater in these families than in those in more affluent circumstances.

With the larger incomes prevalent today, heads of families have been able to purchase insurance in much larger units than formerly. Of its total weekly-premium policies, the Metropolitan is now selling only one-fifth on the lives of adult males. These men are purchasing a substantially greater proportion of their policies on the monthly-debit rather than weekly-premium basis. The smaller of these policies are industrial and the larger ordinary. Furthermore, many of the men are now able to purchase ordinary insurance with premiums payable quarterly or less frequently, and they are doing so. This is evidenced by the fact that, although the Metropolitan sells a great number of policies for very substantial amounts of insurance, about one-half of all its ordinary non-debit policies are being sold for exactly $1,000 of insurance, the minimum amount in this branch. In many cases the wage earners also have the additional protection of group insurance during their working years when their need for it is greatest.

The large combination companies are well equipped to provide appropriate insurance to families of all income levels. The continuing contacts between their agents and their policyholders, coupled with the fact that these agents can offer a complete choice of life insurance policies and services, enable families of modest means to develop and maintain insurance programs that stay in keeping with their needs and circumstances. The industrial branch of the business provides an essential part of this service.

CHAPTER IX

THE GROWING FIELD OF GROUP COVERAGES

By Henry S. Beers, F.S.A.*

Possibly the simplest and most informative way to define group insurance is to say that it is *an employee-benefit plan administered by an insurance company*. This may be said to define group insurance from the end opposite that from which other types of insurance are usually defined; and it is important to do so. What group insurance does for the employee and his family, and what group insurance looks like to the employee, is more important to a true understanding than an acquaintance with the policy forms, actuarial formulas, and legal principles that pertain to this field. On the other hand, you must not get the impression that an employee-benefit plan is a group insurance plan unless it has the usual insurance characteristic that a sum of money (premium) is paid to an insurer in exchange for a promise to pay contingent upon the happening within a certain time of a defined event (hazard insured against).

This short definition covers more ground than the limits of this paper will encompass. In particular, a line of cleavage may be drawn between pension plans and the other kinds of employee-benefit plans that are administered by insurance companies. Frequently group annuities are spoken of as a part of the group insurance category—how important a part is indicated by the statistics that, in the United States during 1948, the insurance companies received some $540 million of group annuity premiums to purchase old-age annuities for almost two million employees, while for group insurance proper the premiums were some $840 million to provide benefits for almost twenty million employees and ten million of their dependents. The line of cleavage is a natural one; group annuities and group insurance do not mix readily. They are harder to discuss together than

* Vice President, Aetna Life Insurance Company.

133

THE O P Q MANUFACTURING CO.
of Easton, West Virginia

Founded 1900   May 1, 1950

To All Employees:

We are pleased to announce that arrangements have been concluded whereby all of our employees may enjoy the benefits of Group Insurance. The A B C Life Insurance Company of Norton, South Carolina, will underwrite the plan.

This insurance will become effective as soon as 75 per cent of our eligible employees make application. The O P Q Manufacturing Company is paying about one-half of the total premium. Your contribution will be deducted weekly from your earnings.

The plan, described on the following pages, has our complete endorsement and we sincerely hope that all of you will take advantage of this valuable insurance protection.

Very truly yours,

O. P. Queue, Jr.
President.

apart. The different types of benefit that go to make up group insurance plans package themselves together easily, while packages that also include pensions are harder to hold together. (An employee asks "What happens if . . . ?" The answer is likely to be "With respect to the pension plan, such and such is the case. For the group insurance, however, the situation is so and so.")

A Particular Group Plan

It has been the author's observation that seldom does anyone achieve a clear idea of group insurance until he has put himself into the position of the employee to whom a group plan is being offered—just as one is not likely to reach a sound critical judgment on any question connected with group insurance without considering how the matter will sound to the employees when it is explained to them.

On the next few pages you will find the text of the specially printed announcement booklet that might be distributed among you, if you were actually the employees of the O P Q Manufacturing Company and we were trying to sell you on the value of signing up to contribute for a group plan. Following each quoted section of the booklet will be found some explanatory comments.

As the following pages are read, it would be well to note how indivisible, or at least how easily packaged, group insurance is. It can be analyzed into sub-categories, such as group life insurance, group disability insurance, group hospital expense insurance, *et cetera,* but the reader will grasp the essence of group insurance more clearly if he reads the employee booklet as a single whole. It is one group plan, even though it provides several different benefits.

Announcement Letter

Considerable attention is usually paid to the matter of making the employee announcement booklet both attractive and readable.

The first inside page is normally devoted to some sort of foreword or letter to employees, such as illustrated on page 134. Often the employer will devote a great deal of thought to the wording of such a letter. Not only can a well-written letter help greatly in persuading the employees to take advantage of the opportunity to subscribe to the group plan but it can also be a valuable factor in employee-employer relations.

When a group plan, whether a new plan being submitted for the first time or a revision of an old plan, is being purchased by the employer as the result of union negotiations, the employer's letter may mention this by saying, "We are pleased to announce that, pursuant to negotiations with ———— Union, Local No. 777, arrangements have been concluded. . . ." Alternatively, the letter is sometimes signed by the union instead of by the employer, or the booklet may contain both an employer letter and a union letter. Other methods that may be followed when group insurance results from collective bargaining are discussed on a later page.

The 75 per cent rule stated in the second paragraph on page 134 is all but universal in group insurance. From the purchaser's standpoint, group insurance is not worth the trouble and expense unless a large majority of the employees want it and, generally speaking, a plan is seldom considered successful if the participation barely exceeds 75 per cent; percentages in the nineties are not at all uncommon and are a much surer indication that the plan will accomplish its main objectives. From the insurance company's standpoint, the acceptance of the insurance by a reasonably high percentage of the eligible employees is necessary to minimize the probability that the worst risks will have accepted the insurance and the best risks refused it to such an extent that the premiums quoted can no longer be expected to cover claims and expenses.

Schedule of Insurance Benefits

The schedule of benefits illustrated on page 138 may be characterized as a "flat schedule" because every employee is offered the same benefits. "Graded schedules" offer different amounts of insurance to different classes of employees, the classification being based on salary rate, occupation, or other appropriate factor.

Under both types of schedules, an individual employee is

offered a particular amount of benefits at a specified rate of employee contribution (unless under that particular plan the employer is paying the full premium). The employee is not offered any choice between a greater and a lesser amount of insurance. This is necessary from the insurance company's point of view, in order to prevent too many of the worst risks from taking the larger amount and too many of the best risks taking the smaller, which might raise the loss ratio too much. In other words, the amounts of insurance offered "must be based upon a rule precluding individual selection," to use a traditional expression.

The illustrative schedule on page 138 is set up as a "package." The employee is offered a list of benefits at a contribution of $2.27 for a single employee, or $4.17 for an employee with a family. He is not offered the choice of taking any one or more of the benefits at an appropriately adjusted contribution rate. In some group plans, the employee is allowed to break the package, but the usual custom is to allow either no breaks or only a few specified types of breaks.

It will be remembered from the employer's letter that the employee contributions are not the premiums charged by the insurance company, but only about half. Sometimes the employer pays the full cost. On the other hand, some plans are paid for entirely by the employees, but this is becoming uncommon, and always has been so in plans including life insurance benefits. (The laws of many states prohibit employee-pay-all group life insurance.)

DESCRIPTION OF THE PLAN

Eligibility

All present full-time employees who are actively working will be eligible for insurance on the effective date of the plan. Employees who are away from work for any reason will be eligible for insurance as soon as they return to active duty.

Employees hired after the plan becomes effective may make application when employed and their insurance will become effective upon the completion of three months of continuous active service.

SCHEDULE OF INSURANCE
BENEFITS

For Employees
Life Insurance	$1,000
Accidental Death and Dismemberment	1,000
Weekly Sickness and Accident Benefit	20
Hospital Expense Benefits	
Daily Benefit for Board and Room	6
Miscellaneous Charges	60
Surgical Fee Benefit—Maximum	200
Medical Expense Benefits	
Office Visit	2
Hospital or Home Call	3

For Dependents
Hospital Expense Benefits	
Daily Benefit for Board and Room	6
Miscellaneous Charges	60
Surgical Fee Benefit—Maximum	200

Employees' Monthly Contributions
Employee with No Dependents	2.27
Employee and Dependents	4.17

The usual rule is that "the plan must be offered to all employees or to all of any classes determined by conditions pertaining to the employment." It is usual to require new employees to serve a "probationary period" of three months, more or less, before becoming insured, but the probationary period is frequently waived for employees in service when the plan is adopted.

Life Insurance

The life insurance is payable in event of your death from any cause at any time or place while you are insured. Payment will be made in a lump sum or in installments to the beneficiary designated by you. The beneficiary may be changed whenever you wish.

If you become totally and permanently disabled while insured and before age sixty, your life insurance will remain in force as long as you remain so disabled, provided proofs of disability are furnished as required. Your contributions toward this insurance cease upon submission of the first proof, which should be filed with the insurance company within three months after total disability has lasted nine months. Subsequent proofs of disability must be furnished each year thereafter.

The life insurance will remain in force for thirty-one days following termination of employment. Within this thirty-one day period, by making application to the A B C Life Insurance Company, you may convert your group life insurance to an individual life insurance policy on any regular plan, except term insurance. This individual policy will be issued without medical examination at the insurance company's regular rates.

The features described above are those customary at the present time. Prior to about fifteen years ago, group life insurance policies usually included disability clauses providing for payment of the sum insured to the employee himself on proof he had become totally and presumably permanently disabled. In times of depressed economic conditions and widespread unemployment, the claim rate under these clauses rose prohibitively, and it proved impossible to restrict payments to those actually disabled in the sense originally intended. While insurance companies have not generally included such clauses in policies issued for the past fifteen years, there is still a good deal of permanent total disability coverage of this nature in force. Many of the policies issued before that time still contain the disability clause and quite a few have increased greatly in number of employees covered or have been extended to new groups of employees.

Accidental Death and Dismemberment Benefits

The accidental death and dismemberment coverage provides benefits for the accidental loss of life, limbs, and sight, including losses resulting from occupational accidents.

The full principal sum to which you are entitled will be paid for the accidental loss of:

> Life (in addition to life insurance)
> Both Hands
> Both Feet
> One Hand and One Foot
> One Hand and Sight of One Eye
> One Foot and Sight of One Eye
> Sight of Both Eyes

One-half the principal sum will be paid for the accidental loss of one hand, one foot, or the sight of one eye.

Payments will be made directly to you, if living; otherwise to your beneficiary.

Frequently this coverage does not apply to occupational accidents, since workmen's compensation laws provide benefits for deaths and dismemberments arising out of such accidents.

Sickness and Accident Benefits

The weekly benefit is payable to you while you are disabled and prevented from working as a result of a non-occupational accident or a disease for which benefits are not payable under the Workmen's Compensation Law.

The weekly benefit to which you are entitled will commence on the *first day* of disability resulting from accident or on the *eighth day* of disability resulting from disease and will be payable for a maximum period of thirteen weeks for any one disability.

If disability is due to pregnancy, the maximum period of payment is *six weeks*. These maternity benefits are immediately effective for all employees whose insurance begins on the effective date of the plan. However, in the case of female employees becoming insured after the effective date of the plan, no benefits will be payable on account of a pregnancy which results in a childbirth or miscarriage occurring within nine months following the date the employee becomes insured.

Payment will be made for as many separate and distinct periods of disability as may occur.

Successive periods of disability separated by less than two weeks of active work on full time will be considered one period of disability unless the subsequent disability is due to an injury or sickness entirely unrelated to the causes of the previous disability and commences after return to active work on full time.

It is not necessary to be confined to your home to collect benefits, but you must be under the care of a doctor during the period of your disability.

This kind of insurance seldom covers occupational disabilities, since they are covered by workmen's compensation laws.

The day on which benefits commence varies from plan to plan. The four most usual arrangements are for benefits to commence on the

8th day for all disabilities,
4th day for all disabilities,
1st day for accidents, 8th day for sicknesses,
1st day for accidents, 4th day for sicknesses.

Benefits almost never commence before the 4th day for sickness disabilities, and seldom commence later than the 8th day for any disabilities.

The maximum number of weeks' benefits payable for one disability also varies. The most usual limit is 13 weeks. Many plans have a 26-week limit. Other limits are less usual.

Premium rates, of course, differ according to the waiting period before benefits begin, and according to the limit of payment.

Most plans provide a maternity allowance of six weeks' benefits. Although plans usually cover pregnancies existing at the time the insurance is originally installed, new female employees are covered only for pregnancies which begin while insured. Sometimes there is no maternity benefit—this would decrease the premium rate, at least for groups containing a substantial percentage of female employees.

Hospital Benefits for Employees

The plan will reimburse you for the actual charges made by the hospital for board and room up to a maximum of $6.00 per day while you are confined as a result of a non-occupational accident or a disease for which benefits are not payable under the Workmen's Compensation Law. These benefits are payable for a maximum period of *31 days* during any one continuous period of disability.

The plan also pays for all charges, other than charges for board and room, made by the hospital up to an aggregate total for any one disability of $60.00 (ten times the rate of daily benefit).

In order to collect these benefits you must be confined for at least eighteen consecutive hours in a legally constituted hospital and be under the care of a doctor. If the hospital makes a charge for board and room, or in cases of emergency treatment for non-occupational accidents, benefits will be paid even if you stay in the hospital for less than 18 hours.

If hospital confinement is due to pregnancy, reimbursement will be made for the actual charges made by the hospital up to a maximum of $60.00, regardless of the number of days of confinement, and regardless of whether the charges are for board and room or other services. In the event of pregnancy, benefits are payable whether the employee goes to the hospital before or within nine months after termination of insurance. However, no benefits will be payable on account of pregnancy if the hospital confinement commences within nine months following the date the employee becomes insured, except in the case of employees whose insurance starts on the effective date of this Plan.

Hospital benefits are payable in addition to any Sickness and Accident Benefits to which you may be entitled.

The plan described is a "reimbursement" plan. There are also "fixed payment" plans, which pay the stipulated daily benefit even in cases where the board and room charges are less, or where the employee is in a free hospital.

Most plans provide daily benefits up to a maximum of either 31 days or 70 days during any one disability. Some plans provide half benefits for a further 120 days.

The allowance for miscellaneous charges (such as operating room, laboratory, X-ray, or anesthesia fees) is usually either five times or ten times the rate of daily benefit, although larger ratios are becoming more common.

The object of the "18-hour" rule is to avoid a large number of small claims, which might increase costs of administration more than real insurance value to employees—also to avoid any tendency to influence employees to go to hospitals for types of treatment normally given in doctors' offices or elsewhere.

Different plans have different provisions with respect to pregnancy or maternity benefits, e.g.:

(i) pay the same benefits as would apply to other causes of hospitalization, but limit the daily benefit to a maximum of 14 days;

(ii) pay up to ten times the daily benefit as reimbursement for board, room, and all other hospital charges;

(iii) pay no pregnancy or maternity benefits.

Surgical Benefits for Employees

The plan pays you a surgical benefit for any operation resulting from a non-occupational accident or a disease for which benefits are not payable under the Workmen's Compensation Law. The amount of payment for a particular operation is shown in the "Schedule of Operations," but if the actual charges by the surgeon are less than that, the payment will equal the actual charges. These benefits are payable whether the operation is performed in the hospital, in the doctor's office, or elsewhere.

In the event that several operations are required, payment will be made for each, but not more than $200 will be paid for all operations during any one continuous period of disability.

Benefits are payable for obstetrical operations whether they are performed before or within nine months after termination of insurance. However, no benefits will be payable on account of obstetrical operations when the delivery or other operation takes place within nine months following the date the employee becomes insured, except in the case of employees whose insurance starts on the effective date of this plan.

Most plans providing hospital benefits for employees also provide surgical benefits.

Several different fee schedules are in use. The schedule on page 148 is one insurance company's "standard $200 schedule." Certain fractions (or multiples) of this table may be used, e.g., for a 50 per cent increase in premium rate, each amount in the schedule would be increased 50 per cent, and the maximum payment for all operations during one disability would be increased to $300.

Obstetrical benefits are sometimes omitted.

Medical Expense Benefits for Employees

The plan pays you for the amount charged by the doctor for medical treatments received during total disability resulting from a non-occupational accident or a disease for which benefits are not payable under the Workmen's Compensation Law. Payment will be made up to $2.00 for each treatment in the doctor's office and up to $3.00 for each treatment at home or in the hospital.

You are entitled to benefits for treatments received on or after the *first day* of disability resulting from an accident, and on or after the *eighth day* of disability resulting from disease. All treatments received on any one day will be considered as a single treatment.

If you are totally disabled for seven days or longer, benefits are available for as many as three treatments received for the same accident or disease within *thirty-one days* after return to work.

The maximum amount payable for all treatments with respect to any one period of disability, including any treatments covered after return to work, is $150, and no benefits are payable after the disability has lasted *thirteen weeks.*

Payment will be made for as many separate and distinct periods of disability as may occur.

Since the surgical fee benefits cover surgical operations, the medical expense benefits are not payable on or after the date of an operation except for treatments given by a physician other than the surgeon who performed the operation. Moreover, no benefits are payable for treatments received in connection with pregnancy or resulting childbirth or miscarriage, or for any dental work or treatment, or for eye examinations or the fitting of glasses, or for X-rays, drugs, dressings, and medicines.

This is the newest of the main group coverages. It is not yet included in many plans, but is growing rapidly in popularity. A considerable variety of plans is available. Some pay doctors' fees only during total disability; some pay regardless of total disability; some pay only during hospital confinement. Some pay beginning with the first treatment for each complaint—others exclude the first few treatments, or exclude treatments during the first few days of each disability.

Dependents' Hospital Benefits

Dependents include a wife, and unmarried children between the ages of 14 days and 19 years.

The plan pays you for the amount charged by the hospital for board and room up to $6.00 for each day that your dependent is confined in the hospital. The maximum amount so payable during any one continuous period of disability is $186.00.

The plan also pays for all charges, other than charges for board and room, made by the hospital while your dependent is confined, up to an aggregate total during any one continuous period of disability of $60.00.

In order to collect these benefits, your dependent must be confined for at least eighteen consecutive hours in a legally constituted hospital and be under the care of a doctor. If the hospital makes a charge for board and room, or in cases of emergency treatment for non-occupational accidents, benefits will be paid even if the stay in the hospital is less than 18 hours.

No benefits are payable for hospital confinement resulting from accidents or illnesses covered under the Workmen's Compensation Law.

The foregoing benefits do not apply to maternity cases. In such cases the benefits are as follows:

Maternity Benefit for Wives—If, while maternity coverage is in force, your wife goes to the hospital as a result of pregnancy, childbirth, or miscarriage, the plan pays you for the actual charges made by the hospital up to $60, regardless of the number of days of confinement.

Maternity coverage does not commence until nine months after your wife's insurance commences but, if her insurance terminates for any reason, maternity coverage does not cease until nine months thereafter.

The benefit amounts for dependents are sometimes the same as, sometimes somewhat less than, those provided for employees. Husbands are sometimes, but not often, included as insurable dependents.

Sometimes immediate maternity coverage is provided for wives insured on the date a new group insurance plan becomes effective; but that is quite expensive (the extra premium charge would presumably have to be paid by the employer, rather than the employees, for reasons that become obvious on reflection).

Dependents' Surgical Benefits

The plan pays a surgical benefit for operations on any of your dependents. The amount of payment for a particular operation will be the same as you would receive, as shown in the "Schedule of Operations." These benefits are payable whether the operation is performed in the hospital, in the doctor's office, or elsewhere.

In the event that several operations are required, payment will be made for each, but not more than $200 will be paid for all operations on a dependent during any one continuous period of disability.

No benefits are payable for operations resulting from accidents or illnesses covered under the Workmen's Compensation Law.

Maternity Benefit for Wives—Benefits for obstetrical operations are payable if the operation takes place while maternity coverage is in force. Maternity coverage does not commence until nine months after your wife's insurance commences, but if her insurance terminates for any reason, maternity coverage does not cease until nine months thereafter.

No Medical Examination

No medical examination is required in order to obtain this insurance if application is made promptly. However, if you do not make application within thirty-one days after you become eligible, the insurance company will require that you furnish satisfactory evidence of insurability, at your own expense, before you can obtain the insurance.

If employees must be actively at work in order to be eligible for the insurance, the proportion with health impairments will be reasonably small. The rules that individual employees may not choose what amounts of insurance to take, and that 75 per cent of the number eligible must subscribe to the plan, give reasonably adequate protection against the danger that the insured group will contain an unduly high proportion of impaired risks. Employees applying some considerable time after they become eligible may be doing so because of some adverse development in their physical condition. Health statements signed by these employees are required in some cases—medical examinations in others.

Insurance Certificate

The insurance company will issue to each insured employee an individual certificate describing the benefits of the plan.

There are normally three documents setting forth the benefit plan:

(1) the announcement booklet, using general language, as understandable as possible to employees;

(2) the group policy delivered to the employer, using (unavoidably though regrettably) very technical language in many clauses, and intended to be the final word in the event of dispute as to meaning or intention;

(3) the employee's certificate, containing his name, the amounts of his insurance, and copies of such portions of the group policy as particularly concern his benefits and the conditions to which they are subject—not easy reading for most certificate-holders, but technically correct and complete; moreover, a moderately ornamental document, as befits

something that in fact ought to be kept carefully amongst one's valuable papers.

Payment of Claims

All claims should be reported immediately to *YOUR EMPLOYER*. Do not wait until you return to work to make your report.
The sickness and accident, and hospital, benefits will be paid weekly and will include payments for fractional parts of a week. All other benefits will be paid promptly upon receipt of required proofs. Your employer has the forms for submitting proof.

Some insurance companies pay claims from their home offices by correspondence. Others have local claim offices in various cities for the investigation and payment of sickness and accident, hospital, surgical, and medical expense claims. Occasionally an insurance company will give a large employer its draft book, so that some designated member of the employer's staff can pay sickness and accident, hospital, surgical, and medical expense claims by drafts on the insurance company.

Termination of Insurance

If your employment terminates, your life insurance will remain in force for thirty-one days. Your other insurance will cease upon termination of employment.
If you are temporarily laid off, your insurance can be continued until the end of the policy month following the policy month in which the lay-off starts. If at the end of that period you are still on temporary lay-off, consideration will be given to continuing your life insurance for a longer period. Continuation of insurance during lay-off will be subject to payment of contributions on or before the pay days on which they would be deducted if you were working.

The restrictions on continuance of insurance during lay-offs, or after termination of employment, are necessary because claim rates are higher during unemployment, and only those who anticipate some claim will be very likely to go to the trouble of sending in their contributions in cash.

Effective Date

The plan will become effective as soon as 75 per cent of our employees apply.

SCHEDULE OF OPERATIONS
Surgical Expense Benefits

ABDOMEN

	Maximum Amount
Appendectomy, freeing of adhesions or exploration of, or cutting into, the abdominal cavity	$100.00
Removal of, or other operation on gall bladder	150.00
Gastro-enterostomy	150.00
Resection of stomach, bowel or rectum	200.00

Two or more surgical procedures performed through the same abdominal incision will be considered as one operation.

ABSCESSES (See Tumors)

AMPUTATIONS

	Maximum Amount
Thigh, leg	125.00
Upper arm, forearm, entire hand or foot	100.00
Fingers or toes, each	15.00

BREAST

Removal of benign tumor or cyst requiring hospital confinement	50.00
Simple amputation	100.00
Radical amputation	150.00

CHEST

Complete thoracoplasty, transthoracic approach to stomach, diaphragm, or esophagus; sympathectomy or laryngectomy	200.00
Removal of lung or portion of lung	200.00
Bronchoscopy, esophagoscopy	40.00
Induction of artificial pneumothorax, initial	25.00
refills each (not more than 12)	10.00

DISLOCATION, REDUCTION OF

Hip, ankle joint, elbow or knee joint (patella excepted)	35.00
Shoulder	30.00
Lower jaw, collar bone, wrist or patella	15.00

For a dislocation requiring an open operation, the maximum will be twice the amount shown above.

EXCISION OR FIXATION BY CUTTING

Hip joint	150.00
Shoulder, knee joint, semilunar cartilage, elbow, wrist or ankle joint	100.00
Removal of diseased portion of bone, including curettage (alveolar processes excepted)	50.00

GENITO-URINARY TRACT

	Maximum Amount
Removal of, or cutting into, kidney	$200.00
Fixation of kidney	150.00
Removal of tumors or stones in ureter or bladder:	
by cutting operation	100.00
by endoscopic means	35.00
Cystoscopy	25.00
Removal of prostate by open operation	150.00
Removal of prostate by endoscopic means	100.00
Circumcision	15.00
Varicocele, hydrocele, orchidectomy or epididymectomy, single	50.00
bilateral	75.00
Hysterectomy	150.00
Other cutting operations on uterus and its appendages with abdominal approach	100.00
Cervix amputation	50.00
Dilatation and curettage (non-puerperal), cervix cauterization or conization, polypectomy, or any combination of these	25.00
Vaginal plastic, operation for cystocele or rectocele	75.00

GOITRE

Removal of thyroid, subtotal	150.00
Removal of adenoma or benign tumor of thyroid	100.00

HERNIA

Single hernia	100.00
More than one hernia	125.00

JOINT

Incision into, tapping excepted	25.00

LIGAMENTS AND TENDONS

Cutting or transplant, single	50.00
multiple	75.00
Suturing of tendon, single	35.00
multiple	50.00

PARACENTESIS

Tapping	15.00

PILONIDAL CYST OR SINUS

Removal of	50.00

EAR, NOSE OR THROAT

Fenestration, one or both sides	200.00
Mastoidectomy, one or both sides: Simple	100.00
Radical	150.00
Tonsillectomy, adenoidectomy, or both	30.00
Sinus operation by cutting (puncture of antrum excepted)	50.00
Submucous resection of nasal septum	50.00
Tracheotomy	50.00
Any other cutting operation	15.00

EYE

Operation for detached retina	200.00
Cataract, removal of	150.00
Any other cutting operation into the eyeball (through the cornea or sclera) or cutting operation on eye muscles	100.00
Removal of eyeball	75.00
Any other cutting operation on eyeball	20.00

FRACTURE, TREATMENT OF

Thigh, vertebra or vertebrae, pelvis, (coccyx excepted)	75.00
Leg, kneecap, upper arm, ankle (Potts)	50.00
Lower jaw, (alveolar process excepted) collar bone, shoulder blade, forearm, wrist (Colles), skull	25.00
Hand, foot	15.00
Fingers or toes, each	10.00
Nose	10.00
Rib or ribs, three or more	25.00
fewer than three	10.00

The amounts shown above are for simple fractures.

For a compound fracture, the maximum will be one and one-half times the amount for the corresponding simple fracture.

For a fracture requiring an open operation with bone grafting, bone splinting, or metallic fixation at point of fracture, the maximum will be twice the amount for the corresponding simple fracture.

RECTUM

Hemorrhoidectomy, external	25.00
internal or internal and external	50.00
Cutting operation for fissure	25.00
Cutting operation for thrombosed hemorrhoids	15.00
Cutting operation for fistula-in-ano, single	50.00
multiple	75.00

SKULL

Cutting into cranial cavity (trephine excepted)	200.00
Trephine	25.00

SPINE OR SPINAL CORD

Operation for spinal cord tumor	200.00
Operation with removal of portion of vertebra or vertebrae (except coccyx, transverse or spinous process)	150.00
Removal of part or all of coccyx, or of transverse or spinous process	50.00

TUMORS

Benign or superficial tumors and cysts or abscesses:	
requiring hospital confinement	25.00
not requiring hospital confinement	10.00
Malignant tumors of face, lip or skin	50.00

VARICOSE VEINS

Injection treatment, complete procedure, one or both legs	40.00
Cutting operation, complete procedure, one leg	50.00
both legs	75.00

OBSTETRICAL PROCEDURES

Delivery of child or children	50.00
Caesarean section	100.00
Abdominal operation for extra-uterine pregnancy	100.00
Miscarriage	25.00

The Insurance Company will determine the amount of payment, if any, for a cutting operation not listed in the foregoing Schedule.

PREMIUM RATES

So far, little has been said about premiums or costs, except to mention that employees usually contribute part of the cost, with the employer paying the balance.

The pattern of premium costs in group insurance is traditionally somewhat different from that in other lines of insurance, although with some possible similarity to participating ordinary life insurance. It has been the practice of the insurance companies to quote group premium rates distinctly higher than expected requirements, at least for what might be described roughly as the medium-sized and larger groups, for average claims and expenses plus an appropriate margin for contingency reserves and surplus or profit. The excess premium collections are then distributed back to policyholders under dividend and experience rating plans. The distribution is called a "dividend" by the mutual life insurance companies. The stock life insurance companies issuing "nonparticipating" policies make their experience rating distributions partly in the form of advance rate credits to reduce renewal premiums, and partly in the form of retroactive refunds, much like dividends, but not so labeled. In addition to paying dividends, mutual companies also reduce renewal rates, but to a lesser extent than do the stock companies.

Dividends or experience rating credits allocated by an insurance company to its individual group policies vary according to the loss experience under the respective policies, and according to their size and the other factors that affect expense rates.

As might be expected, net cost competition among insurance companies is very strong in the group insurance field. Gross premium rate competition has been much less strong. In fact, the different insurance companies have tended to copy each other's premium rates more or less closely. Before the Southeastern Underwriters' decision there was even more uniformity (encouraged by the beautiful romance between Paul and Virginia, not Bernardin de Saint-Pierre's, but 8 Wall. 168). This uniformity has never extended to net costs, in which there has been and is considerable diversity, at least in the details of the different dividend and experience rating formulas, if not in their *average* results. This leads to strong competition, and elaborate and heated arguments before prospective clients as to which company's formulas and practices will probably result in the lowest net cost.

The usual arrangement under a group policy paid for partly by employee contributions and partly by employer contributions is to fix the employee's rate of contribution in advance, letting the employer's share of the premium fluctuate up and down as dividends or experience rating credits fluctuate with varying claim rates and other factors.

If, as sometimes happens in a particular policy, the claim rates and expense charges are so low that dividends or experience rating credits exceed the employer's share of the gross premium, either the employee contribution rates are decreased or the benefits are increased. It is, of course, not contemplated that an employer would ever make a profit from any excess of employee contributions over net cost; in fact, it is not usually considered proper for the employer even to recoup his clerical expenses of administering the plan.

In most cases nowadays, if dividends or experience credits even approach the whole of the employer's share of the gross premium, it is usual for the employer either to reduce the employee contributions or to arrange with the insurance company to increase the insurance coverage so as to re-establish a substantial employer net cost.

Recent Collective Bargaining Developments

For about the first decade of its development, say, from 1912 to 1922, group insurance was adopted by employers from what would today be labeled rather paternalistic motives. In general, the insurance was bought and paid for by the employer and presented to the employees as an act of grace.

During the second decade an increasing proportion of group insurance was offered to employees on a contributory basis, and considerable effort was expended on presenting group plans as attractively as possible. One important objective was that of improving employer-employee relationships. Usually this offer to the employees was made by the employer unilaterally, without prior discussion with the employees or their representatives.

With the last fifteen years' growth in union strength and activity, more and more sales of new group insurance or of increased benefits under present plans have resulted from union pressure. Still more recently, union demands have matured into detailed group insurance clauses in collective bargaining contracts. Actually the precedents for this go back at least as far as a 1926 agreement signed by a trolley car company and its union to provide $1,000 of life insurance and $15 of weekly sickness and accident benefits.

This trend has been strengthened by the Inland Steel and other National Labor Relations Board and court decisions, indicating that an employer whose employees are represented by a union must not act unilaterally, but only after discussion or collective bargaining, in the adoption, modification, or discontinuance of a group insurance plan. In more and more cases we find employee announcements starting out with two letters, one signed by the employer, and one by the union; or with a letter signed jointly by the employer and the union; or with a letter signed by the union alone—all indicating that the group insurance plan represents the conclusion of collective bargaining agreements.

The usual practice, both in cases where the group insurance represents the employer's unilateral offer, and in cases resulting from collective bargaining, is still to have the master group policies issued to the employer. However, sometimes the master policy is written otherwise, e.g., in the name of trustees, one-half to be appointed by the employer and the other half by the union. This technique is being developed particularly for cases where several employers join in a collective bargaining agreement with a union or group of unions.

Developments in the collective bargaining aspects of group insurance are so rapid that it is hard to say today a great deal that will be likely to give a correct picture tomorrow.

History

Group insurance started with group life insurance. Shortly after the first decade of the present century, some (then seemingly ignorant) employers said that they failed to see why a life insurance company could not make a contract with an employer insuring all of his employees, both present and future, according to some formula. After the amount of resistance usual to new ideas, some insurance companies decided to experiment in this field. The companies that did this let themselves and others in for a lot of trouble—believe it or not, some companies now have on their books twice as much group life insurance as real life insurance. Those are extreme instances; on the average, only 19 per cent of life insurance is group life; 16 per cent is industrial; the other 65 per cent is what is called ordinary, i.e., what seventy-five years ago would have been considered the only "real" life insurance.

At the end of 1912, tabulations indicate that twenty-five employers were carrying group life insurance covering about 12,000 employees for an aggregate of $13 million of insurance. That was one-fifteenth of one per cent of total life insurance in the United States. For about the first ten years, group life insurance was something bought and paid for by employers as a gift to employees, usually appreciated, sometimes not—seldom appreciated to the point of justifying the claims of some exuberant salesmen that group life insurance was "strike" insurance, or that its purchase would all but eliminate labor turnover.

By 1922 group life insurance had almost reached the $2 billion mark and covered about 1,600,000 employees. It then represented between 3 per cent and 4 per cent of total life insurance.

It was recognized about that time that group life insurance could be run on a contributory basis with employees paying a substantial part of the cost. An employee contribution of 60 cents per month per $1,000 of insurance became traditional; that was in many instances approximately two-thirds of the average cost, leaving only the other one-third for the employer to pay. Not only was it discovered that group life insurance would work all right on the contributory basis, but it actually seemed to work better. The employees seemed to value more highly something they helped to pay for than something offered them as a gift.

The introduction of the contributory principle in group insurance and the industrial expansion of the 1920's brought group life insurance almost to the ten billion dollar point by 1931. Then the great depression struck. What happened to this new frill in industrial relations, this "unnecessary" investment by a minority of employers in the peace of mind of their employees? There had been some decrease in group life insurance in the business dislocation of 1921—but how did group life insurance stand up during the great depression while payrolls were declining and unemployment mounting? The answer is that it stood up almost incredibly well.

In our table of group life insurance in force at the end of each calendar year, a high point of not quite $10 billion had been reached at the end of 1931. There was an 8½ per cent decline in 1932; another 2 per cent decline in 1933; a recovery by the end of 1934 halfway back up to the 1931 peak; and at the end of 1935 a new high record!

The tragedies of the great depression are not to be made light of, and this story is of no comfort to the dependents of those who lost their group insurance in the great depression. But it is to the everlasting credit of group insurance that it held up during that awful period so much better than did the average payrolls or employment. And so group insurance did something to lessen, rather than to deepen, the gloom of those days.

Since the 1931 predepression high point, ordinary life insurance volume has increased 70 per cent; industrial insurance has increased 80 per cent; group life volume has quadrupled, until it now stands at $40 billion, representing 19 per cent of all life insurance in force. About seventeen million employees are now insured.

It would be wrong to infer from the foregoing that the wave of the future is going to carry group insurance to a height from which ordinary and industrial will look small. Even during group insurance's period of greatest growth, 1938 to 1948, the total growth of life insurance was derived 60 per cent from ordinary, 12 per cent from industrial, and 28 per cent from group.

Group life insurance figures have been used above to try and give an idea of the growth of the group business, because the ancient statistics are reasonably reliable. Statistics for the other kinds of group insurance benefits have only recently been gathered systematically. The present picture is indicated by the following:

Between 1912 and 1948 Group Life Insurance has grown until it now covers seventeen million employees. `

Between 1917 and 1948 Group Disability Insurance (Weekly Sickness and Accident benefits) has grown until it covers about ten million employees.

Since 1935 Group Hospital Expense Insurance has grown until it now covers about eight million employees, a large proportion of whom also insure their dependents under the same Group policies.

Since about 1938 Group Surgical Fee Insurance has grown to cover about seven and a half million employees, of whom a fair number also cover their dependents under the same policies.

Since about 1943 Group Medical Expense Insurance has grown to cover over a million employees and a few of their dependents.

From a slow start during the 1920's, Group Annuities have grown until they are now providing pension plans for about two million employees.

Group insurance is, and will continue to be, a major factor both in the insurance world and in the industrial world.

CHAPTER X

RESEARCH IN AGENCY MANAGEMENT

By Charles J. Zimmerman, C.L.U.*

The first and most obvious thing that strikes us in connection with life insurance is that it serves a broad segment of our population. A recent Federal Reserve study shows that 78 per cent of all spending units own life insurance. This life insurance is widely distributed among these units, being owned by 74 per cent of all units having an income of between $2,000 and $3,000, and by over 90 per cent of all units having an income of $3,000 or more. Approximately eighty million policyholders, paying throughout the current year life insurance premiums estimated in excess of $7 billion, have accumulated more than $50 billion of savings through the medium of life insurance. These savings find their way into every branch of our business and economic life.

From a social point of view, life insurance enables the individual to provide for himself and his family against the hazards of premature death, against the hazards of dependent old age, and against the hazards of economic death through disability. It does this more efficiently than does any other vehicle devised by man. Life insurance enables the individual to underwrite his own and his family's financial independence, thus freeing him from dependency upon the state, or upon the community, or upon some form of charity, whether it is organized or individual. Life insurance contributes to human dignity and human decency. It enables one generation to pass on to the next the accumulated knowledge and the improvement in standards of living upon which the progress of civilization is based. It serves not only the individual but the community and the nation by relieving the community and the nation of the burden of caring for dependents.

* Associate Managing Director, Life Insurance Agency Management Association.

156

Finally, life insurance makes a great contribution to our political way of life. Man has ever sought security. He has also wanted liberty and freedom. Unless he is willing and able to furnish security through his own initiative and his own efforts, he must depend upon the state for it. When man becomes dependent upon the state for security, the state inevitably encroaches upon his liberty and freedom. He therefore forfeits the latter whether the state is communistic, fascistic, socialistic, or paternalistic. All history teaches this lesson. Life insurance is the most effective means by which man can provide security for himself and his dependents through his own efforts. In an industrial and financial economy, it represents "the good earth." It is the author's belief that life insurance is the most effective weapon against encroachment of paternalism. It enables man to do voluntarily what he would otherwise do by compulsion.

Life insurance is big business because life insurance fulfills a big basic need in our way of life. When an individual purchases a sound policy of life insurance, he not only insures his life but he ensures a way of life, and he ensures a continuation of a standard of living.

Role of the Agency Management Association

The Life Insurance Agency Management Association has played a vital role in enabling life insurance to serve better the general public. It is an unique organization, being the only research organization which has been designed and maintained to serve the institution of life insurance of which it is an offspring. This organization came into being in 1921 as an expression of the idea and of the ideals of several outstanding life insurance leaders who believed that the tools of science could be applied to the sale of life insurance. The original organization was known as the Life Insurance Sales Research Bureau. It was supported by six companies which contributed dues in a very modest amount. In 1945 the Life Insurance Sales Research Bureau was merged with the Life Agency Officers Association. It is now known as the Life Insurance Agency Management Association, and is supported by some 200 life insurance companies in the United States and Canada and, indeed, throughout the world. The United States and

Canadian companies represent over 95 per cent of the total life insurance in force in their two countries. Associate-member companies are located in Central and South America, in Europe, in Africa, and in Asia. The Association is a nonprofit organization, located in Hartford, Connecticut. At the present time it has approximately seventy full-time staff representatives.

The Association is composed of four major divisions. Foremost is the Research Division upon which other functions are fundamentally based. Further reference will be made later to its activities. In addition, there is the Company Relations Division which interprets research results to member companies and endeavors to help them put these research findings into practical use. It also interprets the needs and the problems of member companies to the Association. This division is active in the field of life insurance sales management and sales education and training. A third division is known as Institutional Relations. It serves member companies and the institution of life insurance by keeping these companies informed of broad, significant institutional developments both within and without the life insurance business. It maintains close liaison with other associations in the life insurance business as well as organizations outside the business, such as the Accident and Health Conference, and the National Industrial Conference Board. It also has worked closely with governmental agencies in connection with National Service Life Insurance, on-the-job training for veterans, and Social Security. It works in coöperation with colleges and universities in the further development of sound methods of college recruitment by the institution of life insurance as well as in the development of life insurance courses in the colleges and universities. The fourth division of the Association is known as the Administrative Division. It is in charge of personnel, of office procedure, of budgeting and finance, and of internal administration of Association affairs. These four divisions work closely with one another under the supervision of the Managing Director and the Associate Managing Director.

The work which is carried on by the staff of the Association is greatly supplemented by that done by the twenty-one standing committees of the Association, which are composed of representatives of the member companies. Committee members contribute their time voluntarily to the activities of the Association so that it may in turn better serve their member companies.

It would not be possible at this time to touch upon the many activities which the Association, through its staff and committees, is carrying on to improve the sale and the service of life insurance to the public. But we can highlight just a few of these activities.

SELECTION

It was recognized early in the history of the Association that the institution of life insurance could better serve the public if the men in the field were more carefully selected, were better educated and better supervised. Therefore, one of the major and continuing projects of the Association is the improvement in procedures for the selection of men for the sales and sales management end of the business. In order to develop any selection tests which would be helpful in distinguishing men with potential success aptitudes from those lacking these qualities, it was first necessary to define what is meant by a successful agent or a successful manager. Certainly we know that the sale of new business by the individual underwriter or the production of a large volume of new business by the manager is not the sole criterion of success. Such new business must be what is known as *quality* business, namely, business which when once sold remains sold. That in turn means that the business has been sold to fit a specific need of the policyholder. It means that the business remains in force for a sufficient length of time to be of value to the underwriter who sold it, to the sales manager through whose office the business is served, to the company itself, and, most important of all, to the policy-owner.

In 1932 the Association first began to work on the development of an aptitude test for the selection of life insurance salesmen. Much of the early work was done by Dr. A. W. Kornhauser, then associated with the University of Chicago. After a number of years of painstaking research, including the testing of thousands of established agents as well as new agents entering the business, there evolved what is today known as the Aptitude Index. This Aptitude Index is now widely used by the member companies of the Association. Its purpose is to measure the aptitude of the individual for successful life insurance selling.

The Aptitude Index has been in use since 1938. During that time the validity of the Aptitude Index has been continuously checked against the actual results of thousands of men brought into the life insurance business each year. The Association recognized the fact that any selection test must be constantly challenged for validity, and for that reason has continued to conduct experiments for improving the Aptitude Index. It will continue these experiments, and from time to time changes in the Aptitude Index will be made as experience proves that they are warranted.

The Aptitude Index is, of course, not perfect. Nor is it the entire answer to the selection of agents. (No test can be either perfect or sufficient of itself.) The elements of personal judgment are vitally important in the selection of men for any occupation. Furthermore, no test is able to measure all of the factors which are important in predicting future success. Such factors as health and disturbed domestic situations are not measured by an aptitude test. There are, of course, other means of acquiring this information. Nevertheless, the Aptitude Index is of tremendous value in the selection of life insurance agents. Its greatest value lies in its predictive ability to de-select. Under the Aptitude Index system of grading, a man may rate from A to E. Continuous checking of the predictive value of the Aptitude Index against actual results demonstrates without a doubt the fact that those men who rate below B have the odds definitely against them as regards future success in the business of selling life insurance. It is important to bear in mind that the Aptitude Index does not measure intelligence or sales ability in other lines of business, or any other factors; it measures only aptitude for life insurance selling. The Aptitude Index does tell us that, if we are to predict intelligently, we will predict future success only for those men who rate either A or B.

At present the Association is working also on a "selection test" for life insurance managers. This test, which was first developed in 1938, is presently known as the Manager's Evaluation Record. It has not, however, reached the stage of refinement where it has the validity of the Aptitude Index test for the selection of agents. It is important to remember that the development of a selection test for managers is more difficult, due to the fact that there are fewer men by far in management work than in sales work. Therefore, experimentation is limited to a smaller group. Nevertheless, the work in the field of research for the development of a valid test for the selection of managers continues, and with evidence of progress.

As the Association continued to study the validity of the Aptitude Index test for the selection of agents, a second basic factor in the future success of the agent became apparent. It was found that, whereas A and B men enjoyed a greater chance of success, and in fact actually attained a greater degree of success when they entered the life insurance business, there was a great variation in the success of these men as among companies and even agencies. This led to the inevitable conclusion that selection is only one factor contributing to the future success of the individual. A second and most important factor is the *training* given to the individual once he enters the business.

TRAINING

The Association has also been most active in the field of education and training. Today the training courses offered by the life insurance companies are far superior to those offered even a decade ago. Further improvement, of course, can and will be made. The Association's philosophy is that training should embrace everything the manager does in developing agents. Training, therefore, is a continuous process. All companies today have developed good text material for training the new man. Many companies have developed text material for so-called intermediate training to be given to the agent who has been in life underwriting one to three years. Some companies have also developed advanced training material to be given to the agent who has established himself and who has had three or more years' experience in life insurance work.

Paralleling these training developments by the life insurance companies have been similar institutional training programs to which the Association has given its support. For example, in the field of basic training for the new man there are available such courses as are being conducted at Southern Methodist University and Purdue University by the Institutes of Life Insurance Marketing. These have proven to be highly successful, based on the production results and on other success measurements of graduates of these courses. In the intermediate field there is the recent development of the Life Underwriter Training Council. Its courses, conducted over a period of two years, have already shown evidence of contributing to the further improvement of life insurance sales and service. Finally, in the advanced field there is the education and training offered by the study courses of the American College of Life Underwriters, culminating in the attainment of the C.L.U. designation by those candidates who successfully pass the examinations given by the American College. It has been recognized that as the life insurance business has become more complex and as the need of the business for better trained and better educated underwriters has been more widely accepted, the training and educational program of the life insurance companies as well as of the institutional organizations must be improved. Such improvement is being achieved.

Although the business has not made as much progress in the field of managerial training, nevertheless, this Association for more than twenty years has conducted training courses for managers which have been outstandingly successful. In addition, a number of companies have now developed, or are beginning to develop, managerial training courses of their own. But a great deal still remains to be accomplished.

SUPERVISION

In addition to good selection of men and good training of men, there is a third factor which contributes to manpower betterment. That factor is the *supervision* which is given to representatives after they have completed their preliminary formal training courses. In this field, too, the Association has been active.

The most recent study which we have made in the field of supervision developed some very interesting information. In connection with it, we sent questionnaires to 567 men who had entered the life insurance business with an Aptitude Index rating of either A or B, but who had left the business within one year of the time they entered. All of these men had enjoyed better than average production records while in the business. What we were endeavoring to discover was why men who apparently had the aptitude for success and who, in fact, were showing indications of becoming successful, did leave the business.

Replies were received from 261 of the 567 so-called early terminators who received this questionnaire. Although this is a high proportionate return on a questionnaire of this nature, it does not represent a sufficiently high percentage of replies to enable us to state that those replies would be typical for the group of 567 as a whole.

The 261 repliers were most friendly and most frank. All of them still entertained the highest regard for the companies with which they had been affiliated and for the institution of life insurance. They gave various reasons as to why they had left the life insurance business, but three reasons stood out above all others. One major cause which they gave for early termination was that they had received inadequate training in the field. On the whole they were content with the formal office training which had been given them. However, they were of the opinion that, once they actually got into the field, they were neither given sufficient joint work in the field nor sufficient supervision of their field activities. "Give us more field training," they said. Another major reason for early termination was the lack of sufficient prospects on whom to call. Repliers indicated that greater emphasis should be placed upon prospecting, at least in the early training program. The business has always recognized that prospecting is a problem to many men and that it is solved only by those men who recognize the difficulties of prospecting, and therefore make it a continuous process in their operations. A third major reason for early termination was the lack of sufficient cash earnings received. Men pointed out that, whereas they were building up future commissions to be payable over a period of years, nevertheless, the actual cash commissions received and on which they had to depend for immediate living expenses were inadequate. Leaders in the business are in agreement on the fact that we have not made as much progress in the field of adequate scientific supervision of our sales forces as we have made in the field of selection and training of these sales forces.

MORALE

A fourth and final factor determining the success of a life underwriter is the so-called *morale* factor. Even with good selection, good training, and good supervision, a man will not succeed in this business in proportion to his capacity for success unless he has a burning desire to succeed. In our Schools in Agency Management, we ask the question, "Does he want to—enough?"

What is it that makes men want to—enough? One cannot attend a business meeting of any type today without hearing a discussion of the importance of human relations. It is accepted as a fact that where morale is high, men are more easily motivated and stimulated to increase their productivity. Good morale is based in part at least upon sound, strong leadership. This fact impressed the author particularly during his experience of over four years as an officer in the United States Navy during the recent war. That experience took him to many parts of the world and required him to visit many naval stations and to board many ships of the fleet. The tremendous difference in morale among these various units was immediately noticeable even to the casual observer. In all instances where morale was high, it could be traced directly to the fact that leadership was sound, strong, and unselfish. In cases where morale was low, these attributes of leadership were lacking.

The Agency Management Association was quite possibly years ahead of business and industry generally when it undertook its morale studies in 1938. These were completed in 1940, and a series of four booklets based thereon were then issued. In order to gather data for the morale studies, a group of trained interviewers went into twenty life insurance agencies, spending anywhere from three days to three weeks with each agency. These skilled interviewers talked to the head of the agency, his supervisors, his office and clerical staff, and all of the members of the sales force. The interviews were conducted on a confidential basis so that each person interviewed might speak with complete candor and honesty. As a result of these studies, it was concluded that there are three major principles on which high morale is based. First, and possibly most important, is the principle of *individual recognition.* Men want *ego* recognition. They want to be made to feel that they are important as individuals. They want to feel that their jobs are important. The second principle on which high morale is based is that of *personal security*. Men want to know that they will have a job tomorrow, next month, next year, as well as today. They want to know that they are in an occupation in which their earnings will give them a fair return for their effort and for their ability. The third principle on which high morale is based is that of *professional skill*. Men who know their business and who are skillful in the application of their business practices are the men who really enjoy their business.

Job Satisfaction

The Association has also conducted for more than twenty of its member companies what are known as Job Satisfaction Surveys. These surveys, through the medium of questionnaires in which the individuals' replies are protected against any possibility of identification, obtain from sales representatives information as to just what they like and what they dislike about their company's practices, the life insurance business, their managers, their associates, and even their competitors. Job Opinion Surveys, which endeavor to measure attitudes of sales managers toward the same subjects mentioned in the Job Satisfaction Surveys, are another indication of the work which has been done by the Agency Management Association in the field of human relations.

Compensation

The Association has been very active in studying the methods of compensation existent in the life insurance sales field. These methods have changed over a period of years. Extremely large first-year commissions were paid in the early days of life insurance. Gradually, however, there developed a trend toward lower first-year commissions, but with the payment in addition of so-called renewal commissions which generally extended for a period of nine years beyond the first year. Considerable dissatisfaction with this method of compensation was voiced in the 1930's by life underwriters in the field. Their major criticisms were six in number: (1) Too large a percentage of the life underwriter's total compensation was based on new sales and, therefore, on first-year commissions. (2) There was no incentive through compensation for the underwriter to continue to serve his policyholder beyond the tenth year, his commission ceasing at that time. (3) There was very little incentive to serve the policyholder even beyond the first year, except the incentive of making additional sales to that policyholder. This was true because the life underwriter continued to receive his commissions from the second to the tenth year, whether he served the policyholder or not. (4) The life underwriter's income declined as he reached retirement age. He would then be unable because of physical limitations to continue to produce as much business as in his younger years, and there was no pension plan offered by companies to offset this declining income or to provide for the life underwriter at retirement. (5) Income, particularly in the early years of the life underwriter's career, was irregular. Depending on sales volume, an underwriter might have an extremely high income in one month but an extremely low one the next. Underwriters preferred to have these peaks and valleys of income ironed out. (6) The method of compensation did not sufficiently reward the underwriter who wrote good quality business which stayed on the books.

In 1940, the National Association of Life Underwriters, through its Compensation Committee, made certain recommendations in connection with compensation as follows: First, that income be redistributed so as to give greater income to the career agent, i.e., the agent who remains in the business and who writes a good quality of business; second, that service fees for serving the policyholder and servicing the insurance on the lives of policyholders be granted to agents, such service fees to continue as long as the policy remains in force; third, that companies adopt pension plans for their field agents, such pension plans to replace, at least partially, the loss of earning power which would be experienced by the agent as he reaches or passes the normal retirement age of 65. These recommendations, although made by the National Association of Life Underwriters, were based entirely on the studies conducted by the Compensation Committee of the Agency Management Association, on which were representatives of the National Association. Most companies have adopted the recommendations.

There is still some criticism of the methods of compensation. It would be unrealistic to suppose that all men at all times would be entirely satisfied with either the method or the amount of their compensation, but it is entirely realistic to say that great progress has been made in both directions in the life insurance field.

OTHER RESEARCH

The Agency Management Association is conducting research in many other fields. One area of such research has had to do with general agents' compensation as contrasted with agents' compensation. Then there is the study of so-called quality business, or why it is that some policies remain on the books year after year while other policies go off the books within a comparatively short time after they have been sold. Recently we completed in Philadelphia a study of early lapsers, or people who purchased life insurance policies and then dropped them within the first year. It is too early as yet to give you the full results of this Philadelphia Lapse Study, which was conducted with the coöperation of the psychology classes of Temple University. The students in these psychology classes called upon eighty-five lapsers and eighty-five nonlapsers and asked both groups a number of questions as to what motivated them to buy life insurance, how long they had known the agent from whom they bought, how much they knew about the life insurance they bought, and why they had dropped the life insurance if they had done so.

The Association conducts what are known as Buyer Studies. For example, in 1942 we analyzed complete data in connection with over 10,000 policies which had been sold within that year. The purpose of this study was to ascertain what types of people were buying, in what age groups they fell, how they were distributed by income groups, whether they were married or single, whether they had dependents, how they paid their premiums, the amounts of insurance they bought, and many other pertinent factors. Five years later, at the close of 1947, these same policies and policyowners were analyzed in an endeavor to learn which policies were still in force, which had lapsed without value, which had resulted in death claims, and which had resulted in cash surrender, or lapse with value. Much helpful information has been gleaned from this Buyer Study and others which have been made subsequently.

The Association has done considerable research in the field of agency costs in an endeavor to determine what are fair standards for measuring agency costs. The Association publishes a large number of research studies, training material, and other printed matter, such as Manager's Magazine, Manager's Handbook, and sales material. In the future the Association will become more active in the field of market research and market surveys, an activity which has just recently been authorized by our Board of Directors. It would not be possible to cover or even to mention all of the activities of the Agency Management Association, but it would be fair to summarize by saying that the Association has done, is doing, or contemplates doing, research in every phase of the work and activities connected with the distribution of life insurance.

SIGNIFICANT TRENDS

A final word should be said about trends in the business which will have an effect upon its future growth as well as upon the form of its growth. The tremendous increase in taxes, particularly in the field of income taxes since 1930, accompanied by a marked decline in interest rates has made it more and more difficult for the individual to accumulate a sizable estate for himself and for his heirs. For most men, life insurance is the best medium through which they can provide for themselves and their dependents. For many men, it is the only medium available to make such provision. This has resulted in the sale of increasing amounts of life insurance, and in greater emphasis on the type of life insurance which will provide retirement benefits for the insured if he lives, as well as death benefits for his dependents should he not survive to retirement age.

There has also been a trend toward the managerial as opposed to the general agency system. Under the managerial system, the companies have greater management control over their field office managers. The manager is an employee of the company. The general agent on the other hand is an independent contractor. There are advantages and disadvantages to both types of system, and quite possibly a combination of the managerial system with the general agency system will be the most satisfactory solution for most companies in the future.

Certainly there is a trend toward a smaller number of agents in our business, but of higher caliber, with better training, enjoying larger volumes of sales, and hence increased income, and rendering better service to the public. Not only is there greater emphasis upon a smaller number of career agents as opposed to a larger number of full-time agents, but there is a definite tendency to eliminate entirely the part-time agents.

There is a trend toward putting greater emphasis on counseling and less on straight selling in the distribution of life insurance. Life insurance today is sold to fit a specific need of the individual and is arranged to serve best the individual and his family in relation to his general estate, which may comprise both real and personal property. The qualified life underwriter of today must have a knowledge not only of life insurance but of wills, trusts and estates, of the laws of descent and distribution, of the income and inheritance tax laws, federal estate and gift tax laws, of the laws of partnerships and corporations, of business methods and practices, and of many other related subjects. Whereas the life underwriter of today must be primarily a salesman, he must also be a professional man from the standpoint of giving counsel and guidance to his clients and prospective clients.

There is a definite trend toward the sale of life insurance and annuities on either an individual policy or group basis for the purpose of furnishing pensions. The growth in this particular field has been stimulated by the introduction of Social Security as well as by the feeling of insecurity which came to our people during the decade of the 1930's. The growth of life insurance in the pension field will be a continued rapid growth for many years to come. There is also a definite trend toward the sale of welfare group coverages. These coverages include not only group life insurance but group accident and health, group disability, group hospitalization, group surgical, and group medical benefits. Although our nation already is one of the most healthy nations in the world, nevertheless, in certain segments of our population, particularly the middle income class, the misfortune of serious illness or accident is still beyond the ability of most individuals and families to cope with adequately. The solution to this problem lies largely in the field of voluntary prepaid insurance plans to cover these unforeseen and unforeseeable contingencies. In the future, this form of group welfare insurance will become increasingly important in the life insurance picture. It may have some modifying effects upon the agency system and the services of the individual life underwriter as we know them today. However, most students of the business agree that there will always be a need for the services of the well-qualified life underwriter. Human nature being what it is, man will always require the advice and urging of the good life underwriter before he takes the necessary steps to protect himself and his dependents against the hazards of life and living, through the medium of insurance.

It is entirely realistic to predict that life insurance, which has now exceeded $200 billion of insurance in force, will continue to grow at a steady rate in the future. We have not yet begun to insure adequately our human life values. In this respect, the percentage of life insurance as measured against total human resources compares most unfavorably with the percentage of property insurance in force as compared to our material resources. It is the author's conviction that the more our citizens embrace the various forms of insurance, thereby making provision for themselves and their dependents through their own efforts and initiative, the greater will be our success in maintaining those prized gifts—freedom and liberty—which our forefathers fought so hard to attain.

INDEX

Accident and Health Conference, 158

Accidental death benefits, underwriting of, 55

Actuarial Society of America, Transactions of, 52n, 64n

Agency costs, standards for, 168

Agency Management Association. *See* Life Insurance Agency Management Association

Agents:
  compensation of, 124-25, 165-67
  job satisfaction surveys, 165
  morale, principles on which based, 164-65
  selection of, 123-24, 159
    Aptitude Index, 159-61, 62
  supervision of, 162
  training of, 123-24, 161-62

Alcoholics Anonymous, 61

American College of Life Underwriters, 162

American Experience Table of Mortality, 5, 19, 24
  replacement by Guertin legislation, 28

Annual premium deferred annuity, 90-91

Annuities:
  deferred, 86-87, 90-91
  development of, 84-85
  group, 87-88, 91-92
    forms of, 93-94
  immediate, 89-90
  rapid growth, 86
  reserves, 96

Annuity contracts:
  deferred, 90-91
  group, 87-95
  immediate, 89-90

Aptitude Index, 159-61, 62

Aptitude tests:
  aid in selection of agents, 124, 159-61

Atomic Energy Commission, 60

Aviation risks, 60, 61-62

Avocations, problem in underwriting, 62

Best's Life Insurance Reports, 1

Binding receipt, significance of, 75

Buyer studies, 167

Cancer, problem in underwriting, 57

Cardiovascular disease, problem in underwriting, 57

Cash refund annuity, 90

Ceding (original) company, 69

Chartered Insurance Institute, 66-67

Chartered Life Underwriter, 124, 162

Children, underwriting of, 66

Coinsurance, 75-77
  "modified," 77-78

Collective bargaining in group insurance, 152

Colored risks, 63

"Combination" companies, 117-18

Combined Experience Table, 19, 23

Commissioners' Standard Ordinary Table of Mortality, 4, 5, 19, 22, 25, 31, 76

Commissioners' Standard Valuation method, 25

Counseling, trend toward, 169

Creditors, insuring of, 65

Deferred annuities, 86-87, 90-91

Diabetes, problem in underwriting, 58
Disability, occupational. *See* Occupational disability
Disability benefits:
Canadian companies, 108
changes in 1932, 103-4
development in life insurance contracts, 100
prior to 1932, 100-3
subsequent to 1932, 104-7
future developments, 109-10
"indemnity" type, 106
new tables in 1926, 101-2
"presumptive clause," adoption of, 100
reinsurance of, 78
"Standard Provisions" adopted, 102-3
summary of 30 companies, 112-113
underwriting of, 54-55
war service, in case of, 106-7
Dividends:
affected by lower interest earnings, 9
downward trend, 7
group, 150
how some companies solved problem, 10-11

Eastern Underwriter, 42n, 67n
Ecker, Frederick H., 44
Electrocardiograms in underwriting, 59

Federal Reserve Board, 46
Federal Reserve Bulletin, 39n
Friend, Irwin, 39

Group annuity contracts, 87-88, 91-92
deposit administration plan, 94-95
money purchase plan, 93-94
unit plan, 93

Group insurance:
definition, 133
development since 1912, 151
distinguished from group annuities, 133
employee's rate of contribution, 151
growth in all types, summarized, 154-55
history of, 152-55
influence of unions and collective bargaining, 152
net cost competition, 150
premium rates, 150
suggested letter to a group, 134
suggested "plan," 137-47
Guertin Committee, 21, 25, 27
Guertin legislation, 19-32
achievements of, 28-29
nonforfeiture values, 25-28
reserve valuation, 22-25
situation in 1948, 30-32
uniformity aspect, 20-21

Harrison, G. L., 34n, 42n
Heart diseases, problem in underwriting, 59
Houghton, Claude, 30
Housing, 44n
Hunter Disability Table, 100
Hypertension, 59
effect on mortality, 59

Illinois Standard Valuation method, 25
Immediate annuities, 89-90
Impairment study 1929, 57
Industrial life insurance:
agents, selection and training of, 123-24
amount in force, 115
amount paid in benefits, 116
beneficiary, 120
conversion privilege, 120
disability benefits, 116
endowment policies, 116
expenses incurred, 130-31

Industrial life insurance—*Cont'd*
  family programming, 125-27
  field force organization, 122
  health and welfare programs,
    129-30
  lapse rate, 128-29
  nonforfeiture values, 121
  plans of, 127
  policy provisions, 118-20
  practice prior to 1920, 117
  premium accounting system,
    122-23
  risks, selection of, 121-22
  settlement options omitted, 118
  wage-earners' insurance, trend
    in, 132
Inland Steel case, 152
Institute of Life Insurance, 16, 54
Insurable interest:
  basic for sound insurance, 48,
    54, 63
  definition of, 64
Interest rates:
  decline in, 1
      causes for, 41
      corrective measures taken, 3
      effect on anuity contracts,
        95-97
      effect on life insurance in-
        vestments, 40
      effect on policy loans, 17
      impact on new policies, 3,
        14-15
      impact on old policies, 6-7
      impact on settlement op-
        tions, 14
      results of, 9
      significance of, 1
  downward trend ended, 18
  fixed rate prescribed, 23
Investments of insurance compa-
    nies. *See* life insurance invest-
    ments

Job Opinion surveys, 165
Job Satisfaction surveys, 165
Joint and survivor annuity, 90

Jones, Homer, 39, 42n
*Journal of the American Associa-
    tion of University Teachers
    of Insurance*, 42n, 43n
*Journal of the American Society
    of Chartered Life Underwrit-
    ers*, 98n
*Journal of Business of the Univer-
    sity of Chicago*, 42n
Journal of Commerce, The, 44n

Kornhauser, Dr. A. W., 159

Laird, J. M., 64n
Life Agency Officers Association,
    157
Life annuity, 89-90
Life insurance:
  growth in 47 years, 33
  importance as a social institu-
    tion, 20
  industrial. *See* Industrial life in-
    surance
  its mission, 156-57
  investment trends, 35
Life Insurance Agency Manage-
    ment Association:
  Administrative Division, func-
    tion of, 158
  buyer studies, 167
  Company Relations Division,
    function of, 158
  compensation, study of, 165-66
  Institutional Relations Division,
    function of, 158
  Job Satisfaction surveys, 165
  Research Division, function of,
    158-68
  result of a merger, 157
  role in life insurance, 157
Life Insurance Association of
    America, 35, 40
Life insurance investments:
  common stock, 42
  equity-type, 37
  importance in American capital
    markets, 33

Life ins. investments—*Cont'd*
  other, 36-44
  preferred stock, 41
  rental housing projects, 43
  trends, 35
  United States Government securities, 35
Life Insurance Fact Book, 16, 33n, 35n, 88n
Life Insurance Investment Research Committee, 42n
Life Insurance News Data, 43n
Life Insurance Sales Research Bureau, 157
Life Insurance: Trends and Problems, 2
Life Underwriter Training Council, 162

McClintock's Annuity Tables, 85
Maine, R. F., 42n, 43n
Managerial system, 168-69
Managers:
  Evaluation Record, 160
  training of, 161-62
Manager's Handbook, 168
Manager's Magazine, 168
"Manchester Unity" Sickness Tables, 101
Married women, underwriting of, 66
"Modified coinsurance," 77-78
Mortality:
  among annuitants, 98-99
  effect of under- and overweight, 57
  influencing factors, 50-51
  method of determining extra, 53
  new table, 28
  range of classification, 48
  reduction in recent years, 56

National Association of Insurance Commissioners, 21
National Association of Life Underwriters, 166

National Industrial Conference Board, 158
National Labor Relations Board, 152
National Service Life Insurance, 158
Nationality, problem in underwriting, 62-63
Nerlove, S. H., 42n, 43n
Nonforfeiture values:
  Elizur Wright sponsored, 25
  new statutory measure, 27
  provision in industrial policies, 121
  unique American product, 25
Numerical rating method, 52-53

Occupational disability:
  covered by workmen's compensation laws, 141
Occupational underwriting, 60
Old Age and Survivors insurance, 88
  proposed extension, 111
  dangers involved, 111, 114
Oriental race, mortality among, 62-63
Our National Debt and Life Insurance, 41n

Parkinson, Thomas I., 42n
Pension trusts, 88-89
Philadelphia Lapse Study, 167
Policies, life insurance:
  costs compared, 15
Policy loans, affected by lower interest rates, 17
Premium and dividend scales:
  1929 and 1948 compared, 8
Premiums:
  adoption of higher scale, 3
  annuity, 95
  cause of increase, 5
  provisions for extra mortality, 53
Prospecting, 163
Purdue University, training program, 162

Racial background, problem in underwriting, 62-63
Reder, M. W., 38n
Refund annuity, 90
Reinsurance, life:
accounting methods, 80
amount at close of 1948, 83
"coinsurance" plan, 75-77
contracts, types of, 73
definition, 69
"en bloc" or "assumption," 82
fraud, in case of, 82
"indemnity" reinsurance, 82
plans in use, 75-76
retrocession contract, 74
"risk-premium" (yearly renewable term) plan, 75-76
rules governing, 79
settling death claims, 81
trends today, 83
two classes of, 72-73
Reinsurer, 69
Reserves:
bases for determining amount, 22
Commissioners' Standard Valuation method adopted, 25
origin of fund, 22
strengthening of, 11-12
sums involved, 12-13
Retention limits, 70
position of small company, 71
special class of applicants, 71-72
Risks, selection of:
alcoholics, 60-61
army and navy personnel, 60
aviation, 60, 61-62
cancer, 57
cardiovascular disease, 57
colored race, 63
diabetes, 58
factors in evaluating, 50-51
foreign groups, 62
heart diseases, 59
hypertension, 59
moral hazards, 61
numerical rating, 52

occupational hazards, 60
purpose of, 48, 50
racial background, 62
substandard, 48
superstandard, 47
tropical diseases, 61
tuberculosis, 57-58
ulcers, 59
"Risk-premium" (yearly renewable term) reinsurance, 75-76
Rogers and Hunter, 52n

Selection of risks. See Risks, selection of
Settlement options:
affected by interest rates, 14
guarantees in new policies, 14-15
problem in old policies, 16-17
Shepherd, Bruce E., 36n
Single premium deferred annuity, 90
Smith, B. H., 42n, 43n
Social Security, 158
Old Age and Survivors insurance, 88
Southeastern Underwriters' Association, 150
Southern Methodist University, training program, 161
Spectator Company, The, 83
Standard Nonforfeiture and Valuation Legislation, 19
Supreme Court, 1944 decision, 21
Surplus:
amount maintained by life companies, 12
change in 20 years, 3
transferred to reserves, 11-12, 13
Survey of Current Business, 38n, 39, 40n

Tables, 2, 8
Tax system:
effect on equity investments, 40
Temporary National Economic Committee, monograph, 42n
Texas City disaster, 60

Tropical diseases, problem in underwriting, 61
Tuberculosis, problem in underwriting, 57-58

Ulcers, problem in underwriting, 59
Underwriting:
  accidental death benefits, 55
  children, 66
  creditors, 65
  disability benefits, 54-55
  duties involved, 47
  group insurance, 55
  industrial insurance, 55
  investment income, 66
  key man, 65
  married women, 66
  nationality problems, 62-63
  non-medical, 55
  occupational, 60
  principles, summary of, 54
  racial problems, 62-63
  reinstatements and changes, 55
  valuing earned income, 64-65
  X-ray and cardiograms, use of, 59
Unique Manual-Digest, 2
United States Government Bonds:
  investment in, by life insurance companies, 35
United States Treasury, 46

Veterans Administration, 58

Whittaker, Edmund B., 55n
Wilson, Jean, 44n
Workmen's Compensation Law, 140, 141, 143, 145
Wright, Elizur, 23, 25

X-ray, use in underwriting, 59

Yearly renewable term. See "Risk-premium" plan